Weekend Mechanic's Guide to Peak Performance and Handling

Weekend Mechanic's Guide to Peak Performance and Handling

Bill Farlow

TAB BOOKS
Blue Ridge Summit, PA

Trademarks

Compu*Coil is a trademark of Jacobs Electronics.
Dura-Spark is a trademark of Ford Motor Company.
HEI is a trademark of General Motors Corporation.
Autotronics is a trademark of Chrysler Corporation.
Firebird is a trademark of Pontiac Motor Division, General Motors Corporation.
Marvel Mystery Oil is a trademark of Marvel Oil Company.
Lubrigas is a trademark of L.G. Formulators.
Teflon is a trademark of Dupont Corporation.
Slick 50 is a trademark of Petrolon Corporation.
Craftsman is a trademark of Sears, Roebuck and Co.

FIRST EDITION
THIRD PRINTING

© 1989 by **TAB BOOKS**
TAB BOOKS is a division of McGraw-Hill, Inc.

Library of Congress Cataloging-in-Publication Data

Farlow, Bill.
    Weekend mechanic's guide to peak performance and handling / by
Bill Farlow.
        p.   cm.
    Includes index.
    ISBN 0-8306-1980-1   ISBN 0-8306-3180-1 (pbk.)
    1. Automobiles—Maintenance and repair.   2. Automobiles-
-Performance.   I. Title.
TL152.F34   1989
629.28′722—dc20   89-32258
                                                                        CIP

TAB BOOKS offers software for sale. For information and a catalog, please contact TAB Software Department, Blue Ridge Summit, PA 17294-0850.

Questions regarding the content of this book should be addressed to:

Reader Inquiry Branch
TAB BOOKS
Blue Ridge Summit, PA 17294-0850

Acquisitions Editor: Kimberly Tabor
Technical Editor: Peter D. Sandler

Contents

Acknowledgments

No book is the result of only one person's work. My name may be listed as the author, but the book could never have been written without the help of many people. Kim Tabor, the editor who talked her editorial committee into approving the book, deserves special recognition for her courage. My mechanic friends, Jack Klamm and Bruce Chaffee, answered more questions than anyone should be asked. The authors and publishers of hundreds of books studied over a lifetime made contributions that I could not begin to list.

Growing up on a farm during the era known as the Great Depression gave me an opportunity to learn the self-sufficiency that comes from doing your own repairs. My father will never know how much I appreciated his willingness to let me learn even when the learning sometimes meant lost wrenches and stripped threads.

No spouse should ever have to live through the agonies of a first book. Special thanks are due to my wife, Karen, for her indulgence.

Introduction

The old theory is if you can understand how something is supposed to work you can repair it. It never was completely true, but I believe understanding is essential to making good repairs and modifications. That's why this book deals with more theory than some readers might want. I've never felt satisfied with simple, step-by-step instructions that omitted the explanations.

At a time when repairing or modifying a car or a light truck is more difficult than ever, I believe that it has never been more important that we undertake the job. Too many of us spend our working hours at jobs that reduce our feeling of worth. One way to regain a sense of our importance as an individual is to make some part of our lives individualistic. Modifying a car is an excellent way to say to the world, "I'm here and I have a special car to show for it. By my efforts, this car runs better than when it left the factory. It's uniquely mine."

"Spam Cans" is a derogatory term applied to small airplanes that seem to be alike whether made by Cessna, Piper, or Beechcraft. The term might well be applied to the products of Ford, General Motors, and Chrysler, too. It's sometimes difficult to tell them apart from across the street.

If you're tired of being lost in the crowd, if you're tired of driving a "Spam Can," this book's for you. In it I show you how to take whatever car you own, boulevard warrior or family cruiser, and put your own performance mark on it. You will learn how to make it handle the way you want it to, not the way some committee of engineers in Detroit decided it should. You will learn how to improve its performance without sacrificing its smooth-running characteristics. If better mileage or more power are your goals, you'll find answers here. If you want sources of information so that you can go further, you'll find help in the Bibliography.

You will be happy to learn that you don't have to be a professional mechanic to use what you learn here. My assumption is that you have had little or no experience with a wrench but are willing to learn. I've kept explanations simple so that you don't need a lot of background to understand and use the information. You won't have to spend a fortune on tools, either. You probably have some already. The rest you can buy as you need them. You will find that tools pay for themselves in repair bills saved. You will also find that tools, your skills, and the information given here will help you build a better car than you started with.

Even if you never intend to lift a wrench, this book is for you. If you drive or own a car or light truck, sooner or later you will have to have it repaired or serviced. Those are requirements that come with ownership. Too many times cars are taken to a mechanic with sketchy descriptions of some malfunction, and the mechanic is told to fix it. (My favorite example is an acquaintance who frequently described her car as "running heavy." Neither her mechanics nor I ever figured out what that meant.) The mechanic might be as honest as Abe or he might be the biggest con artist since Barnum, but the car owner might never know. He'll just pay the bill and wonder. With the information in this book you'll have a better notion of how to describe malfunctions and how to evaluate the mechanic's work. You'll also know how to tell him what modifications you want if you decide to hire the work done.

The purpose, then, of the book is twofold. I want to give you information that will help you modify your car so that it is uniquely yours and I want to help you better understand how the different systems work. Either way, you'll know more about your car or light truck and save money. You might even develop a new hobby.

1
CHAPTER

What Good Handling Is

DESCRIPTIONS OF HOW A CAR HANDLES AND WHAT *HANDLING* MEANS VARY AS widely as driver's experiences. The words, "This car handles heavy," are not only ungrammatical, but useless. What do you mean by *heavy*? For that matter, what does *handling* mean?

HANDLING IS A SUBJECTIVE MATTER

Handling refers to a vehicle's responses to the road surface, the ambient wind, the load being carried or towed, and the driver's control inputs. Some cars, because of their design compromises, tend to wallow as they respond to unevenness in the road. Others move from side to side in response to the wind or draft from passing trucks. Most drivers find such behavior annoying. In some instances, it can be dangerous because of its unpredictability. Predictability is one important factor in the handling of any vehicle.

For many years the cars from one large manufacturer were noted for their soft, wallowing ride. The fact that their cars were so popular indicates that there are widely varying tastes in handling. I found driving those cars uncomfortable. Millions of other drivers were not bothered. Was I wrong? Not necessarily.

The factors that constitute good handling are subjective. Some drivers— I'm one—prefer a firm, controlled ride. I want to feel the road, rather than have it disappear under the car. I want the car to respond instantly to any movement of the steering wheel. In other words, I want to know that I am controlling the car, rather than just going along for the ride. I will describe a car with those characteristics as having good handling.

1

A hot rodder might want something different. He is likely to be willing to accept an even firmer ride than I do. Or he might be so interested in powerful performance that he ignores poor handling characteristics.

If the hot rodder's interests take him into the area of racing sprint cars as an example, his ideas of handling become even more specialized. The sprint car shown in Fig. 1-1, and many other classifications of race cars, are built to travel forward in a more or less straight line and turn left. Right turns are not part of its driving requirements. Try to drive it on the highway at even legal speed limits, and control problems will become very obvious. But the owner would say his car had excellent handling. And it does, for its specialized use.

It also requires some structural parts that most of us would find unacceptable on a street car. The fins and wing shown in the illustration would seem out of place on the street. Under many circumstances, such as in a strong cross wind, they would be dangerous. But the racer finds them essential. Those fins and wings contribute to good handling for the race driver, but they would seriously hamper handling for the street driver.

The driver of dragsters is very concerned with handling. In less than eight seconds his car might rocket from a standstill to well over 200 miles per hour in a distance of a quarter mile. His main concern is keeping the car moving in a straight line while the rear tires slip from side to side in response to changing road surfaces. He has no interest at all in the way the car handles in corners. He turns no corners.

Fig. 1-1. This sprint car represents one extreme in handling requirements. It is designed to go very fast on tracks with left-hand turns. Its handling characteristics would be totally unsuitable on the street.

John Q. Citizen, out for a ride with his family, turns corners, lots of them, both left and right. Usually he is not interested in being able to take corners at maximum velocity as is the sports car or circle track racer.

But there is a wide variation in the way so-called family cars handle in corners. Some roll badly. Others exhibit extreme oversteer or understeer. One car might be able to take a corner safely and comfortably at 60 miles per hour. In another car, that corner would feel unsafe at 40.

The drivers of so-called sporty cars (Fig. 1-2) expect handling to be firm but comfortable. They want a minimum of roll on corners, no wandering down the road, and quick response to driver input.

The van shown in Fig. 1-3 is set up to pull a travel trailer weighing 10,000 lbs. The driver of such a rig has his handling requirements, too. He is probably not interested in making quick turns at high speeds, because he needs to control not only the truck but a trailer that weighs 10,000 lbs. or more. That trailer presents a large area for the wind to blow against. Often the result is a trailer that tries to steer the truck. Good handling for the driver of such a combination means, at least in part, resistance to the effects of wind.

It also means predictable behavior when you're applying brakes and negotiating downhill mountain curves. Good handling means predictable behavior when making emergency maneuvers in response to other drivers' actions.

Predictability is one definition of good handling. You want a car or truck that is not going to give you any unpleasant surprises. You want to know that you are in control.

Fig. 1-2. With minor modifications, you can quickly improve the handling characteristics of this sporty Trans-Am.

Fig. 1-3. A van such as this one is intended for hauling or towing heavy loads. With its high center of gravity it can never handle like a sports car, but it can be improved by careful selection of shocks, antiroll bars, and tires.

STEERING WITH MINIMUM CORRECTION

Driving a car, any car, requires attention and energy. Before the nearly universal use of power steering, driving required much more energy than it does today. But even power steering takes energy. If your car wanders around the road because of poor response to the road surface or wind, driving it requires a lot of attention and continual steering correction. After several hours you become tired. A tired driver is not as safe as one who is fresh.

So you can say that for good handling the car has to be stable, not wandering on its own. If it shows too much interest in setting its own course, you are not in control. Your attempts to reestablish and maintain control might give your arms and shoulders lots of exercise, but the gym is a better place for developing muscles. You want a car that steers easily but waits for your steering input.

Driving is not all in a straight line. Sooner or later, probably sooner, you come to a corner. As you turn the steering wheel into the corner you might notice that the car is slow in responding, that it seems to take more input than it should. That kind of response is called understeer. A car with understeer seems not to turn as sharply as the movement of the steering wheel would suggest.

As Fig. 1-4 shows, the rear wheels tend to move inside the radius of the turn, requiring more movement of the front wheels than expected. In a car with understeer the driver automatically sets the steering wheel for what he thinks is the correct amount of turn. As the car enters the turn the driver notices that he needs a little more steering effect and instinctively makes the correction.

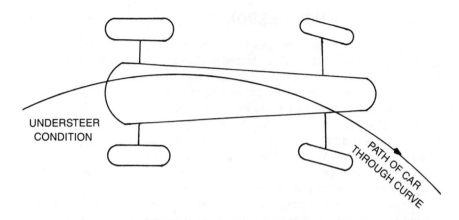

Fig. 1-4. This diagram illustrates the path of a car's wheels through a corner showing under-steer. Note that the rear wheels track inside the curve of the corner.

With a car showing understeer, corrections are instinctive. Designers consider that to be safe. Most cars are designed to have a certain amount of understeer.

But suppose that the car does just the opposite. You set the wheel for the expected turn. As you enter the turn the rear of the car tends to swing outside the radius. You immediately sense that less turning force is needed and back off the steering wheel a bit. But centrifugal force has already begun to take effect, swinging the rear of the car further out requiring less and less steering wheel force. The result can very quickly be that the car turn ends in a skid. Figure 1-5 shows the forces at work. A car that tries to turn more sharply than steering wheel position would indicate has oversteer and is considered unsafe in normal operation.

Good handling requires that a car have a small amount of understeer rather than oversteer. Except for some types of racing, no car should exhibit over-steer.

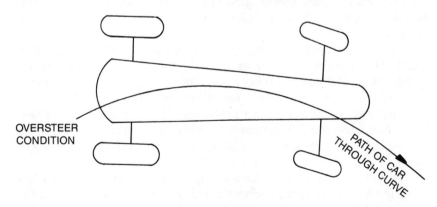

Fig. 1-5. This illustration shows a car with oversteer. The rear wheels track outside the curve of the corner. A car with oversteer can be dangerous on the road.

GOOD EMERGENCY RESPONSE

Not all drivers are as careful as you. Sometimes they force you into taking emergency avoidance action. Or an animal or object suddenly appears in front of you. You need a car that makes emergency maneuvers safely.

When the steering wheel of a car moving at high speed is suddenly turned, centrifugal force and inertia tend to keep the car moving straight ahead. Since there is a less than solid connection between the car body and its wheels and chassis, the straight-ahead force is experienced as body roll. Body roll is one factor in understeer. When you are trying to avoid an object in the road, you don't want a lot of body roll or understeer. Neither do you want your evasive maneuver to quickly turn into an off-road adventure.

When evasive action is needed, it's needed right now. A split second later is too late. Good handling in emergency maneuvers means complete controllability. Before power steering became so popular it was common to build in easy steering by selecting a steering gear ratio that required as many as six complete turns of the steering wheel to go completely from one side to the other. Quick, sharp turns were nearly impossible. Evasive steering action required more turning of the steering wheel than you could accomplish in the amount of time available. Steering was just too slow.

For fast emergency maneuvers you need a car with fast steering, little body roll, and a small amount of understeer.

BUT YOU HAVE TO BE ABLE TO STOP

There are three factors in good braking performance. First you must be able to come to a complete stop in as short a distance as is possible while maintaining control. Stopping distance is important. Ask the guy in the hospital bed whose car would have stopped in just 20 more feet. I distinctly remember bumping a car in a chain reaction accident with enough force to do several hundred dollars' damage. Another six feet of space and there would have been no problem.

Since the first automobile, engineers have worked to make cars stop more quickly. Most readers are too young to believe it, but early cars had only two-wheel brakes. That might have been sufficient when speeds were low, but no one cried when we got brakes on all four wheels. Next came hydraulic brakes, a huge improvement over the former mechanicals. Recently we got disc brakes on the front wheels, and on all wheels of some cars. Even more recently, engineers developed brakes with anti-locking systems to avoid having any wheels skid.

That's the second factor. It does little good to stop from 60 miles per hour in 100 feet if you end up going backwards in the next lane. Part of the problem is that the weight of the car tends to shift forward when brakes are applied. The result is that most of the braking power is in the front wheels. As the rear wheels become lightened, there is less friction between the rear tires and the pavement. Too much braking effect on the rear wheels will lock them up.

Wheels that are no longer turning generate little friction against the road surface. With the front wheels generating lots of braking force and the rear wheels generating little, the result is an uncontrolled skid into the next lane. You are lucky, no one else is there and there are no large, solid objects.

Maximum braking force is generated when the wheel is just at the edge of being locked up. Keeping those wheels turning is extremely important. Antilock brake systems use a variety of methods to sense when the wheels are stopping and release the brakes very slightly to get them rolling again. The balance point is a very fine line and changes with dozens of factors. A few of these are weight of the vehicle, distribution of that weight, condition of the tires including pressure, type of rubber used in the tires, condition of the road surface, and nervousness of the driver.

Brake engineers have studied many different types of brake friction materials in an effort to develop the best. Until recently most brake shoes and disc pads were formulated largely from asbestos with other materials used as binders and modifiers. Asbestos was little affected by the heat resulting from braking action and showed good wear characteristics. It was also inexpensive. With a variety of binder materials asbestos could be manufactured in almost any shape.

But asbestos has one very negative characteristic. When asbestos dust is inhaled it often leads to lung cancer. Employees in factories manufacturing brake materials and mechanics who repaired brakes were unavoidably exposed to asbestos dust. Even using water to remove the dust when doing a brake job was not adequate protection. The federal government has removed asbestos as a material for brakes as well as for insulation, its more common use.

Brake linings and disc pads now are made from a variety of materials, some natural and some manufactured. In spite of all the compromises involved, each company believes it has the best material.

A vehicle in motion represents a huge amount of energy. That energy can be considered as stored in the vehicle. Stopping the vehicle requires that the energy be converted to another form since one of the basic laws of physics is that energy is not destroyed, but is simply converted. Brakes are a way of converting that energy to another form, heat. An emergency stop from 60 miles per hour results in a tremendous amount of heat. That heat is all concentrated in a very small area, the contact point between the brake friction material and the drums or discs.

When metal is heated it expands. In the case of drum brakes, such as those still used on most rear wheels, that means the drums get slightly larger. As they get larger additional brake pressure is required to force the brake shoes that much farther out.

Also, as the friction materials get hot they begin to release gases from the binding material and the friction material. The gases tend to act as a lubricant between the friction materials and the brake drums. Not good. The lubricating action requires still more pressure, which creates more heat requiring additional pressure. If the brakes get hot enough they reach the point where additional pressure has no effect, and you get the feeling that you have lost your brakes.

That's the third factor. The condition is called brake fade. Engineers have worked for years to eliminate the effects of brake fade. One result has been disc brakes. Because of their design disc brakes not only permit much greater pressure to be generated but also do a better job of dissipating the heat into the air. That's why they are so popular. All cars, vans, and light trucks today use disc brakes on the front where most of the braking power is generated. Some more expensive models also have them on the rear wheels.

REASONABLE RIDING COMFORT

Good brakes and predictable steering are important parts of good handling, but there is another factor that must be considered. If the car rides like a log wagon because it is too stiffly sprung, it will be no fun to drive. You'll probably also get strong comments from your navigator in the right seat.

Lots of car owners have the notion that stiff springing is a necessary part of good handling. Part of that comes from the factories' habit of including stiffer than normal springing as part of their handling packages. Those packages do help. But some drivers succumb to the good old American belief that if a little is good a lot is better. When it comes to springs and shocks, that just isn't true. If it were, we could just eliminate springs entirely. That's what increasing spring power ultimately means.

BETTER HANDLING MEANS FUN DRIVING

Fun driving is a lot more than all-out speed and rocket power. Driving the Indianapolis 500 seems like the ultimate thrill for those of us who have never had the chance. Most 500 drivers would agree it is quite a thrill. But by the time they have reached the 300-mile mark, many of them would prefer to be in a Jacuzzi with a tall, frosty glass of refreshment. Driving with that kind of power and at that speed requires a degree of attention that most of us can't give. It's just plain hard work.

It also is painful. Those cars are not very comfortable to ride in. They are designed for one thing, to go very fast on tracks that have only left-hand turns. A comfortable ride is far down the list of priorities.

Driving should be fun. That means a combination of car and driver that becomes one being. In a car that has good handling, miles and hours tend to disappear with minimum effort. Driving becomes a matter of thinking the car around turns and through the traffic.

A car with a mind of its own, one that requires constant attention and seems intent on beating your backside, is a menace. It is a danger to you and everyone else on the road. It is no fun to drive.

Designing a car that offers ideal handling for all types of driving is not possible. That's why the number of family cars seen in the Indianapolis 500 is very small. That's also why there is an equally small number of Indy cars found on the highway. Designing any kind of car is a series of compromises. One purpose of this book is to help you decide what kind of car you want and to help you make those compromises.

2
CHAPTER

What Do You Mean, Good Performance?

It would be easy for all of us if we could give a set of time and speed parameters and say that constitutes good performance. But just as we found out in the last chapter on handling, it isn't so. Good performance, like good handling, means different things to different drivers.

GOOD PERFORMANCE IS SUBJECTIVE

When I was an 18-year-old leadfoot with only cars and girls on my mind, my taste in both was much different from what it is now. We won't talk about girls. At that time I wanted the fastest, most powerful car in the county. Those were the only two requirements for good performance. Fuel consumption was very low on my list.

Now I'm more than slightly over the hill. I still like speed and power, but I've come to realize that there are a number of other factors that have to enter the equation. One of those is fuel cost. Gasoline now costs about five times as much as it did in those halcyon days. In recent years the cost was as much as eight times what I paid back then. Those high prices will soon be with us again.

There are ways of getting speed and power and reasonably good mileage, of course. Depending upon how you balance the three factors, the cost can be mild to wild. Fortunately for your wallet and mine, good speed, moderate increases in power, and good fuel economy can be had without a second mortgage on the house.

COMPROMISES, COMPROMISES

The automotive world is full of people who would have you believe that you can't increase the power of an engine without sacrificing fuel economy. They say that increased power demands an increase in the amount of fuel burned. That used to be the conventional wisdom, but it does not have to be true. For example, I drive a van that is used in the summer to pull a travel trailer. Because we spend a lot of time in the mountains and I hate having to push the rig over the top, I want lots of power. One way to get it is to use a large engine. I've got one, a 460 Ford. Those engines have a well-earned reputation for brute power and an appetite to match. That is especially true if the van is geared for pulling. Mine is.

But the modifications I have made have not only significantly increased the power output; they have also increased my fuel mileage by a whopping 28 percent. And it didn't cost a bundle. Can you do it, too? Perhaps I was lucky, but there is no reason why you can't do even better.

There are lots of other examples of vehicles with high power. The muscle cars of 20 years ago are still popular. If you don't believe it, just price a Mustang or Camaro or Firebird from the late 60s. Those cars have done an excellent job of retaining their value. Today the engineers are finding ways to build another series of muscle cars—for a price. Their popularity is proof that lots of drivers still want performance.

Examples abound. Figure 2-1 shows one. This class of car looks as if it's going fast even when standing at the curb. But its looks are not empty. This car,

Fig. 2-1. Unless a sporty car such as this one has good performance the owner will be disappointed. The car looks fast and powerful and should exhibit those characteristics.

as well as others built on the same idea, delivers excellent acceleration and very acceptable economy.

Not everyone wants or can use a sporty car. Some owners prefer cars such as the one illustrated in Fig. 2-2 for their own good reasons. But even though this car is relatively heavy and would never find its way to a drag strip, it can easily be made to offer the excellent acceleration and handling that will make it a safer and more satisfying car to own and drive.

Visit any shopping mall parking lot or travel any street and the word "turbo" will be commonly seen. Turbochargers are so accepted that nearly every manufacturer has at least one series of cars equipped with them. Even superchargers, once the sure sign of a die-hard hot rodder, are finding their way into factory models. Both devices are easy ways for engineers—and you—to increase the power of an engine by an easy 50 percent while maintaining or improving fuel mileage.

Until very recently an engine with more than two valves per cylinder was a rarity except for sophisticated racing engines. Now four valves per cylinder are expected in a performance engine. There are only two reasons for designing an engine with four valves per cylinder. One is that to some people the design becomes a prestige item. Owning that kind of engine gives you something to talk about. But the big and only legitimate reason is that additional valves improve the power output of the engine. That's the only reason the engineers care about.

The name of the game today is power with economy. That's a huge change from even ten years ago. Ten years ago you sometimes would have had difficulty in finding the power of an engine mentioned in advertising materials. Power was

Fig. 2-2. The owners of family sedans such as this one can expect that their cars will deliver lively performance even though they will never be serious entries in a race.

a dirty five letter word because it implied excessive fuel consumption. Now, with smaller but more muscular engines we can have both power and fuel economy without feeling guilty.

But there are more wimps than muscle cars on the market. Part of that is because of the cost of muscles from the factory. Part of it is that some drivers don't want or need performance. And some drivers, like you, would prefer to buy the less expensive wimp and give it a muscle transfusion. Let's admit it; it is fun to have a car that everyone thinks is a Clark Kent but has a hidden heart of Krypton. It is a lot more fun to have transplanted that heart yourself through the suggestions and ideas given in this book.

Building a car that has good performance but doesn't cost a mint is fun. It's also quite practical. There are lots of things you can do that cost very little or nothing and can result in more power and better fuel economy. There are more that cost a little or a lot. Depending upon how much you are willing and able to spend, you can use aftermarket manifolds, heads, ignition systems, cams, gear changes, and supercharges that will cost as much as the car and convert your Clark Kent into a real Supercar. One of the questions you have to decide early in the game is what you want your car to do. Another is how much you are willing to spend.

There is a huge performance industry just waiting to hear what you want them to send. You can buy anything from hotter ignition systems to performance carburetors to manifolds (offering better breathing) to superchargers to complete engines. All will change your car's performance. Some, such as the

Fig. 2-3. A supercharger such as this one is an easy and certain way to turn a wimp into a charger if the installation is done correctly.

supercharger and engine shown in Fig. 2-3, will give significantly greater power. Others, if you make the wrong choice, will give you an engine totally unsuited for street driving. The point is that what you want is available for a price, but you can make the wrong choice and waste your money if you don't know what you are doing. Don't worry; by the time you have finished this book you will know the right choices to make.

REASONABLE ACCELERATION

Let's start talking about what you want your car to do. You probably don't need or want the kind of acceleration that a top dragster delivers. For one thing, those cars bear almost no resemblance to a street car. Another point is that they are far from legal on the road. A third is that the cost of getting that kind of acceleration is difficult to imagine.

There are, of course, street cars that are run in their own special classes at the drag strips. Even most of those leave a lot to be desired in everyday traffic driving. I'll get around to some of the reasons why a bit later.

So the question is, how much acceleration do you want? The 0 to 60 miles per hour time is one of the measurements given in nearly every car test reported by the magazines. Because of timing, driver ability, and manufacturing variations, no one knows what the current winner is. But the numbers give opportunity for lots of street corner arguments about the "best charger" at the moment and undoubtedly cause much drooling among those drivers whose cars don't come close.

Building a winner for the stoplight grand prix isn't difficult if that's all you want. Take almost any car in good mechanical condition and drop in a set of high numerical gears, something in the 5.50 to 1 area, and you can get a stoplight screamer. But that car is good for little else. Fuel economy would be abysmal. Engine life would be short. Proving that you're top gun would get you enough paper from the police department to cover a wall. And replacing tires would cost a mint.

One problem of having a stoplight screamer is that you have little else. That means you will continually have the urge to show what you do have. The police will become very interested in your activities and rightly so. The streets are no place to race.

Building a car only for acceleration doesn't make a lot of sense for most of us. But we do need to be able to blend with traffic at the freeway ramp, or we become a hazard. Often that blending requires better acceleration than most performance wimps can offer. There are also the frequent occasions when the maneuvers of some airhead place you in jeopardy if you don't move quickly. In the previous chapter I talked about good emergency maneuvers as an essential part of good handling. Some of those maneuvers require muscular acceleration to avoid becoming a statistic in tomorrow's paper.

But how much acceleration is needed? Too much for the handling characteristics of your car, and you become the problem. Balance is essential. That means a careful balance of both performance and handling. It also means a balance of your car and you. Don't buy more acceleration than you are absolutely certain you can handle.

Acceleration improvements translate into power increases. There are several ways to increase power. You can bolt on intake manifolds and install performance camshafts. Exhaust headers usually help. Adding a supercharger is certain to give an increase in power. Or you can buy or build a full-race engine. But be careful. You may find that what you get is not what you want. There are some characteristics of high performance engines that are not so desirable. For one thing, race engines are hard to start, and they don't idle at the speeds you normally think of as idling.

STARTS EASILY AND IDLES WELL

If you've ever had the opportunity of watching pit activity at a race, you've seen that starting a race engine is somewhat different from starting your everyday street warrior. The racers often use special, high-powered external starters with either several batteries or 220 volt power. They also are never started at 20 degrees below zero. Your situation is different. Your car has to start in all kinds of weather to get you to work or to make an important run to the supermarket. You also would be somewhat limited if you depended upon an extension cord to furnish your starting power.

And listen to those race engines once they do start. Sound a little fast? You're right. Idle speed for racers might well be higher than your fastest freeway cruising speed. That's because they won't run at a slower speed. With their concentration on top end power, bottom end performance is totally sacrificed. In effect, they have thrown away most of the engine that you need.

Look at the catalog of any of the companies that make and sell performance intake manifolds and camshafts. Read the specifications for their products. Notice the engine speeds that each is intended for. One that I'm looking at mentions that it is intended for engine speeds of 1,500 to 6,000 revolutions per minute (rpm). Another by the same company is designed for engine speeds of 6,500 to 10,000 rpm. The first one would be a good choice for a street car. The second would be a disaster. In selecting your modifications, remember that you will spend more time than you want at idle speed and slightly above. Remember, too, that depending upon the gearing you select, your engine will seldom see speeds above 4,000 rpm.

Another thing to remember is that you will sometimes need help in getting your car started. Regardless of how well you maintain an engine and its related systems, there are going to be times when it doesn't want to start. If you call the local motor club, will they help you? If you have an engine too heavily slanted toward racing, they won't. Let the tow truck driver see a supercharger poking its head through the hood, and he probably won't even stop. On the other hand, if he happens to be another gearhead he may give you special attention—but don't depend on it.

So, more compromises.

SMOOTH THROTTLE RESPONSE

One of the most irritating experiences for a performance minded driver is to punch the accelerator and have the engine respond by asking, "Say wha'?" It also can be dangerous when the situation calls for you immediately to be somewhere else. A too frequent complaint from owners of recent models is flat spots in the car's response. You've probably experienced it yourself. Sometimes it occurs just off idle. More frequently the flat spot will be at moderate engine speed. Wherever, it is more than just a nuisance.

The change from carburetors to fuel injection systems has eliminated most of the flat spot response. But flat spots are not a necessary characteristic of engines with carburetors. With proper selection of modifications you can make your engine deliver smooth, instant response at all speeds.

Just as predictability is important in good handling, it is important in good performance. Driving is not fun if you can't be sure what your car is going to do. An unpredictable car is dangerous. One of the reasons you want to modify your car is to get rid of those areas where performance is not dependable.

FUEL ECONOMY

I know of no driver who is not affected by fuel cost. At the time of writing, gasoline in my area is running $.93 to $1.09 a gallon. Just a few years ago it was up to $1.50. As much as we might like to dream of a continuing supply of cheap gas, the prices are going to go back up. The only questions are when and how high. Even at $.93 the cost of fuel is not inconsiderable.

Bashing the federal government and its mandates for increasing fuel economy has become a popular sport among automobile aficionados. Many writers are fond of saying that fuel economy would have increased just as much without governmental intervention. They claim that competition between the companies would have produced the same or better figures. Frankly, I doubt it.

Average gasoline mileage has more than doubled within the last 10 years. It is common to find the top mileage cars each year offering figures in the 50 to 55 miles per gallon (mpg) range. Some are even higher. Ten years ago cars of equal size had mileage figures approximately half that. As an example of mileage achieved in the dim past and lack of economy increase, I offer a bit of personal experience. I had a 1948 Studebaker that routinely gave 25 mpg in highway driving. Later I had a 1960 Ford Falcon of almost the exact same size engine and weight that gave 26 mpg under the same conditions. Twelve years of competitive improvements gave one mile per gallon. By 1988 a Ford Tempo of nearly the same specifications is giving 32 mpg. Not a tremendous difference, is it?

But there are big differences. Gone are the behemoths of the 50s and 60s that gave only six and eight miles per gallon. Present is a whole class of cars—such as Escorts, Hondas, Reliants, and Corsicas—that routinely deliver 40 or more mpg. Also present is a new class of cars that give performance equal to the muscle cars of pleasant memory with greatly improved fuel economy. These new rockets have engines about half the size of their ancient cousins and deliver three times the gasoline mileage. Not bad.

Perhaps even more importantly, all of these successes are with gasoline that would have been considered very low quality 20 years ago. Add to that fact that the new cars are helping to give us cleaner air for more healthful breathing. I think the engineers have accomplished a lot. Would all this have happened without the government's none too gentle insistence? Doubtful.

Each new requirement for emissions reduction and mileage increase was met by screams of "Foul" and "Impossible" from industry officials. It would be naive to believe they would have changed voluntarily.

The requirements for mileage increases represented official recognition that gasoline supplies were limited. Whatever the optimists believe, there are limited amounts of crude oil available. Eventually it will all be gone. As supplies diminish, the cost of getting the remaining amounts will skyrocket. Requiring mileage improvements is the government's way of postponing the inevitable end of petroleum-based gasoline. I am no lover of governmental intervention, but this time they were right.

The point of all this is that you can have a high performance automobile and still maintain good mileage and clean emissions. This last, clean emissions, is important. Removing the antipollution equipment from your engine is not only illegal; removal is neither necessary nor desirable. We must have clean air, or we can't breathe. And you can have a powerful, economical engine with all its antipollution equipment intact.

There are several ways to get the extra power. Some owners will select refinements such as performance manifolds and camshafts. Others will be satisfied with improved ignition systems or exhaust headers. Some will want combinations of these and other bolt-ons. And a few will go for the ultimate muscle transfusion, a supercharger. There are advantages and disadvantages to each of these approaches. In the following chapters I will discuss what is available and what you can expect it to do. First we'll talk about tools.

3
CHAPTER

Tools You'll Need

ONE FINANCIAL HAZARD OF WORKING ON YOUR OWN CAR OR TRUCK IS THAT
you'll need to buy some tools. The flip side is that doing the work yourself will
save you more than the tools cost. Quality tools will literally last almost forever.
I have some that my father bought probably more than 60 years ago. My sons
will eventually get some use out of them.

WRENCHES

A variety of wrenches will be needed in different types and sizes. If your
vehicle is an older model, most wrenches needed will be in the old standard
sizes. Newer models require metric sizes. Unfortunately, there are some
models that use both metric and standard.

The wrenches used most frequently are box and open end wrenches. Box
wrenches have six or twelve point openings shaped like rings at each end to fit
hexagonal nuts and bolt heads. Six point wrenches are slightly stronger, but
twelve point wrenches permit greater flexibility in tight quarters. I've never
broken a twelve point wrench.

Open end wrenches have a roughly U-shaped opening. They are made for
use on square nuts and should not be used on hexagonal nuts because they tend
to slip on the small bearing surfaces.

Combination wrenches are the same size at both ends with one end open
and the other end box. Noncombination wrenches have a different size at each
end. For example, one end might be ½ inch and the other end ⁹⁄₁₆ inch. There
are advantages to each type. I have a few of each, but most are not combination
type.

Box end wrenches are usually offset with a slight angle between the end and the handle. The offset permits room to grip the wrench when you're working on nuts against a broad, flat surface. Some offset wrenches have a greater angle for more clearance. I've not found these to have any great advantage.

In standard size wrenches, you will need to cover ¼ inch up to 1 inch in both box end and open end types. In metrics you will need from 6mm up to 19mm. If you do much work on shock absorbers and spring shackles, a couple of larger sizes will be needed. Check the sizes as you need them. These larger wrenches get a bit expensive. You can buy the wrenches one at a time as needed or you can buy a set. Buying the set can save as much as 50 percent of what you pay with single purchases.

There is a special type of end wrench that should be in every mechanic's kit. This is the flare-nut wrench used on fittings on fuel lines, fuel pumps, and carburetors. Flare-nuts are made of brass and are soft. Using an ordinary open end wrench often results in a ruined fitting. The flare-nut wrench looks like a box end wrench with a notch cut in the box to permit the wrench to fit over the tubing. They come in sets of three to handle the common sizes.

SOCKET WRENCHES

Socket wrenches are very convenient because they can be used with a ratchet handle or a breaker bar. The ratchet handle permits work in close quarters. The breaker bar is a long handle used to break loose a nut that has rusted tight. You can also use sockets with a flexible joint or an extension between the handle and the socket. Both are very useful features. Sockets will be needed in the same sizes as your other wrenches.

A socket will have two openings, one square and the other hex. The square opening is the drive side and will usually be ¼ inch, ⅜ inch, or ½ inch to fit a corresponding square key on the drive handle. Small sockets up through ½ inch are most conveniently used with ¼-inch drive. Larger sockets work best with ½-inch drive. Adapters are available to use the ¼-inch drive sockets with ½-inch drive handles. If you buy sockets in sets—the cheapest and most convenient way—you will get a variety of useful handles and extensions with the set.

You will need to buy a special spark plug sockets for ½-inch drive to fit the size spark plugs in your engine. Spark plug sockets are available plain or with a flex joint. The flex joint will be very convenient.

If you do much engine work, a torque wrench will be necessary. A torque wrench is really a long socket drive that registers the amount of force being used. Most engine nuts, and some others, should be carefully tightened to a prescribed force. The only accurate way to do this is with a torque wrench.

ADJUSTABLE WRENCHES

Adjustable or crescent wrenches are the modern equivalent of the monkey wrench that came with early Fords. Available in different lengths, they have adjustable openings. Many mechanics scorn their use with good reason. Adjustable wrenches are notorious for slipping and rounding the corners of nuts. Yet, they are almost indispensable in some situations. Buy good quality and use them carefully. I use two sizes, 10 inches and 12 inches.

While not an auto mechanic's tool, a pipe wrench will find a lot of use in your tool kit. Don't use it on nuts; it will destroy the surfaces. One about 18 inches will be most useful.

Another special wrench you will need is an oil filter wrench. One type has a large, dished surface that fits over the end of the filter and is turned by a socket drive handle. Another is a weird looking wrench that resembles a metal strap with a handle. The strap fits around the filter, and you tighten it by operating the handle. The strap type will work well on most engines, but there are some that have such limited access to the filter that only the other type can be used. Check your engine and get the wrench that seems to be needed.

ALLEN WRENCHES

Allen wrenches are pieces of hexagonal steel shaped like the letter L. They are available in several sizes to fit cap screws with socket heads and set screws. Get a set in either standard or metric sizes, whichever is needed for your vehicle.

PLIERS

Pliers are probably the most misused tool in anyone's kit. Although they are very valuable, pliers are not wrenches and should never be used as a wrench. The temptation to do so is great, but the risk is greater. Just when you're sure they won't slip and round the shoulders of a nut, they do. The best rule is never to use pliers for a wrench.

But pliers do have important uses. You need a small diagonal plier for cutting wire. A slip-joint plier about six inches long is handy for a variety of gripping tasks. Two arc joint pliers, six inches and thirteen inches, are very versatile. A small needle nose pair and a larger long nose pair of pliers are necessities. Medium size locking pliers make a handy small vice.

I like pliers with plastic-covered handles. They are warmer in cold weather, less likely to slip in your hand, and they offer some electrical insulation. Cheap plies are worse than useless. The joints don't fit well. Cutting edges are frequently misaligned. Good quality pliers, like good quality tools of any type, are a pleasure to use and last much longer.

SCREWDRIVERS

Fortunately, you won't need as many different size screwdrivers as wrenches. There are three types of screwdrivers. The most common type is the flat blade. You will need ones with blades ⅛ inch, ¼ inch, and ⅜ inch wide in a variety of lengths. Be sure you have at least one stubby ¼-inch blade.

The other two types are the cross-bladed screwdrivers, Phillips and Reed Prince patterns. They are very similar with the most obvious difference being that the Reed Prince blade has a sharp point. The Phillips head is the more common of the two. I suggest one of each of the three sizes.

Traditionally, screwdriver handles were made of wood. Wood is still frequently used, but plastic has become much more common. The advantage of plastic is that it does not become oil-soaked. Plastic handles are a good insulation from the high voltages found around spark plug wires and distributor leads.

Screwdrivers should never be used with a hammer except for a possible light tap to free a rusted screw. Screwdrivers don't make very good pry bars either. Because I know you will need a light pry bar, I suggest a very heavy screwdriver about 15 inches long. But remember that it is only for light prying. Get a small pry bar, or wrecking bar, for heavier use.

GAUGES

Many people believe that new spark plugs are set at the factory for the proper gap. That isn't possible because of the variety of engine applications for each plug. Furthermore, if you follow the suggestions in chapter 7, you will need to try a variety of gaps to find the one best for your engine and the way you drive. Get a spark plug gauge that ranges up to .080 inch. A good gauge will also have small slots that can be used to bend the outer electrode of the plug to change the gap.

Feeler gauges are thin pieces of steel for measuring clearances in some kinds of engine and tune-up work. They are not properly used for setting spark plugs. Get a small set, and keep them clean and free of rust.

Probably the least respected gauge used around a car is a tire gauge. Most people believe that the gauge that is found on many pressure hoses is adequate. Not so. Those gauges get so much abuse that they rarely indicate accurate pressure. Get your own tire gauge, and treat it carefully. There are two types of tire gauges, the dial type and the pencil type. The dial type is the more accurate but is easily damaged if it is dropped. A quality pencil type gauge is adequate. Use it regularly and your tires will pay you back with less wear and better gas mileage.

Vacuum gauges are invaluable for tune-up work and diagnosis of engine problems. In addition to the small one permanently mounted on your dash, you need a large one for shop work. They are not expensive but worth far more than they cost.

TIMING LIGHTS

Timing lights are used to set the ignition advance. When properly hooked up to the engine, they flash each time spark is fed to the timing cylinder, usually number one. The flash is aimed at the engine's timing marks. When the light flashes it makes the timing marks appear to stand still so that they can be read.

The light is also used to check the operation of both the centrifugal and vacuum advance systems of the distributor.

The best timing lights are the set-back type. These have a dial that is turned until the timing marks appear to line up. Then the dial is read and indicates the amount of advance that is present. If that is not the amount wanted, adjustments are made to the distributor. Full and clear instructions for use come with the light.

Timing lights are available at parts stores, catalog outlets, and discount stores. Your mechanic will buy a heavy duty model because he uses it a lot. I don't use mine that much. I bought it at a discount store. It might not have the quality and sturdiness required for constant use, but it is adequate for casual use.

JACKS AND STANDS

In spite of the tire companies' claims of immortality for their tires, tires do go flat. Even if they didn't, they would need regular rotation from one wheel to another to equalize wear. A jack is needed to lift the wheel.

I'm sure that the jacks that come with cars are designed and built by demented little gnomes who gleefully think up ways to frustrate motorists. What other explanation can you have for such devilish contrivances as bumper jacks? If they don't let the car fall at the most inopportune moment, they twist the bumper out of shape. Or they don't work. Somewhere near Portsmouth, Ohio, there is a bumper jack that I tried to throw into the Ohio River about two o'clock one morning. May it rest in peace.

Scissor jacks are a vast improvement over bumper jacks. They are much more solid, more dependable, and just as easy to operate. Even though I prefer a hydraulic jack for most situations, I have to admit that a scissor jack can be used in less space when the tire is completely flat and every part of the car seems to be even with the ground. Get one with at least 3,000 lbs. capacity. Store it with a piece of ¾-inch plywood about 10 inches square that will be used as a firm platform when the ground is soft.

For heavy duty work there is no jack equal to a good hydraulic jack. With a capacity of four tons or more, it will find many uses around your shop. A good hydraulic jack can be used in a horizontal position as well as in the more conventional vertical position for applying pressure to straighten bent pieces of iron or move an engine over slightly. Considering the precision needed in their manufacture, hydraulic jacks are a bargain.

Whatever kind of jack you use, never crawl under a vehicle that is supported only by the jack. Holding up one corner of the car with your chest while you try to maneuver yourself out from under it can ruin your disposition. The answer is a good set of sturdy jack stands. Since your life is on the line, there is no such thing as spending too much for jack stands.

Some people like the metal ramps sold through catalogs and at auto discount shops. After demolishing one ramp, I built my own out of pieces of 2 × 8 lumber securely nailed together to form a platform with one end tapered for a ramp. You won't demolish these quite so easily. Ramps are good for holding up the vehicle when the wheels don't have to be removed. Just be absolutely certain that the wheels are blocked.

THE QUALITY DECISION

Few of us can make a purchase without considering the price. The question of what quality of tools to buy is bound to come up. Having bought a few tools at the bargain counter, I've come to the realization that most bargain tools are no bargain. There are significant and important differences in the quality of the materials used and the construction. Quality wrenches fit better. That translates to fewer ruined nut surfaces and fewer skinned knuckles. A wrench that ruins a part that costs five times the price of the wrench is no bargain. A screwdriver with a poorly shaped blade that tears up a screw head, necessitating an expensive removal technique, is no bargain. Quality tools last longer and help you do a better job.

Another factor in buying quality is that most name-brand tools have a guarantee that means something. As an example, a Craftsman tool from Sears, Roebuck is guaranteed for the life of the tool. If it breaks, take it back to the store for an immediate replacement. That's also true of other well-known brands.

More subjective is the matter of user satisfaction. Quality tools simply feel better in the hand. Any craftsman will tell you that using a good tool is much more satisfying than using an inferior product. Save your money by spending a little more and buying tools with a recognizable brand name.

Within some lines of tools there is a choice of professional or hobbyist quality. Supposedly, the professional quality tool is made with greater precision from sturdier materials. That's probably true. If your tools are going to get a lot of use, buy professional quality. Your grandchildren will thank you for it when they finally inherit the tools. If your use of a particular tool is casual and if the hobbyist quality carries a full replacement guarantee, then hobbyist quality may be adequate.

TOOL BOXES

I have a sizable collection of toolboxes that are too small. They sit empty on a shelf as a reminder that tools are like rabbits; they multiply. Except for special situations where it is essential to conserve space, small toolboxes are a waste of money.

I now have two boxes that get regular use. One is 18 inches long with two drawers and a top compartment. The other is considerably larger. The small box is filled with the tools most commonly used and stays in my van. With those tools I could do almost any job on the van. Some tasks would require using a less than optimum tool, but I could manage. That's my portable tool kit.

The other box is mainly used for storage of larger, less frequently used tools. It's big and heavy and not well-divided, but it serves its purpose well. If I were going to be traveling in the van for several weeks, it would go along.

Toolboxes are made of either steel or plastic. Steel rusts; plastic does not. Plastic is strong but not as strong as steel. I haven't seen a plastic box with pullout drawers. Some plastic becomes brittle and easily broken at low temperatures. Steel has no temperature problems. Both of my boxes are steel, but I have one small plastic box that contains the metric wrenches used on my motorcycle and my wife's car. I'm sure that as we become completely metricized I'll have to have another steel box to hold the needed metric tools.

Keeping your tools organized makes work easier. Drawers and trays facilitate organization. I use one drawer for wrenches other than sockets and the other drawer for screwdrivers. Pliers go with the wrenches. A wire stripping tool and allen wrenches are with the screwdrivers. Sockets and gauges are stored in the top compartment. Spare nuts and bolts are stored in a small plastic container in the top. By having a space for everything and being certain that each tool goes back into its space, I know where to look when I need a tool. Since no one else uses my tools—a very important rule—I have no one but me to yell at when a tool is misplaced.

SERVICE MANUALS

The water pump on your car is in the process of mugging itself, and you hate having to pay a mechanic to replace it when you believe you can do it yourself. But you're not sure where to start. You know you could replace the ignition module yourself—if you just had a little information. Replacing the shocks should be an easy do-it-yourself job; but which end should be removed first? Or does it make any difference?

Doing your own maintenance and at least light repairs makes sense in saving money. It also makes sense in getting you more familiar with your car or truck. Even if you aren't going to do the work yourself, you can save money and steer clear of unnecessary repairs if you know what goes on mechanically with your car. And often you can find a problem while it is still small and inexpensive if you know what to look for. Having the right information can also help you decide which jobs are beyond your ability. That can save you money, too.

Even though you have had a lot of mechanical experience, specific information is often needed to make those repairs or do that maintenance. Well, good news! The information is easily available. There is a wealth of repair manuals available, and they don't cost more than the repair. Some of them you can get from the company that built your car or truck. Some of them you can buy at your nearest bookstore. Many of them are available at your local library.

There are independent companies that publish manuals for nearly every car or light truck built in the last 30 years. Which is better, the company manual or the one from an independent? That's not so easy to answer. It depends on you, your mechanical ability, and what you want to do. Factory manuals are written for the mechanics in local dealer repair facilities. A high level of expertise and experience is assumed. That doesn't mean that you wouldn't find them useful, however. One big problem with factory manuals is that they are written in the year the vehicle is built. As the vehicle is used by thousands of buyers, problems arise and solutions are found. The solutions find their way back to the dealers through service bulletins. Unless you subscribe to the service bulletins, you'll never get that new information.

Independent publishers approach manuals a bit differently. Their manuals are designed to cover a span of several years and are updated annually. As modifications are made and new service procedures established, the changes appear in new editions of the manuals. That can be a real help for most of us.

Independent manuals fall into at least two general classes. One group, exemplified by Chilton's popular series, deals with a particular make and model. For example, Chilton has a volume for Ford vans covering all years from 1961 to 1988. There are similar volumes for nearly every make and model of car and light truck sold in the United States. This series of manuals has very complete step-by-step instructions for repairs and tune-ups of all systems and components. Also included are complete specifications and capacities for the models covered. In addition to repair and tune-up instructions there are sections of general interest such as ways to improve economy and suggestions on purchasing tools. Only a moderate level of expertise is assumed. They are available in most book stores for less than $13.

The other type of independently published manual covers a class of vehicle or chassis for all manufacturers for a span of several years. The best known are *Chilton's Car Repair Manual* and *Motor Auto Repair Manual*. Both cover all makes of cars. Both are updated annually. Both have highly detailed specifications and clear step-by-step instructions for replacement and adjustment of components. Most operations are illustrated with very clear drawings. Neither manual includes wiring diagrams. The Chilton manual has separate sections on repairing such mechanical components as air conditioning, electrical systems, emissions systems, carburetors, steering, transmissions, and differentials. The Chilton manual also has an excellent trouble-shooting and diagnosis section. Both manuals assume a fairly high degree of expertise but certainly not beyond that of a skillful amateur. They are available in most bookstores for less than $30. They can also be found in most libraries. I grew up with a *Motor Manual* and continue to find the new editions useful.

You might want to take a look at the appropriate factory repair manuals. Illustrations are clear, as are maintenance schedules and service locations on the chassis. I found the instructions for replacement of components less detailed than either the Chilton or *Motor Manuals*. There are good diagnosis suggestions for most systems and common problems. There is a section on servicing electrical components but no wiring diagrams. Wiring diagrams for most models are contained in a separate volume. These manuals can be found in some libraries. You can also order them through your local dealer. There should be ordering information in your operator's manual—if you got one. Factory manuals cost from $15 to $100 depending upon what is covered and the method of distribution.

Which manual is best for you? As I said earlier, that depends on you and what you want to do. I have come to depend upon the Chilton series for one make and model. But I would always want to have the appropriate volume of

Motor Manual available. If you look in dealers' repair shops you'll find factory manuals, of course. If you look in independent garages you'll find a few factory manuals and a lot of Chilton's and *Motor Manuals*. I strongly suggest you look at all of them before making your purchase.

Using service manuals can be very interesting and productive. If you do your own maintenance and light repair work, you can save lots of money that can be spent on other things.

4
CHAPTER

Shock Absorbers and Antiroll Bars

SHOCK ABSORBERS AND ANTIROLL BARS ARE DEVICES ADDED TO YOUR CAR TO improve both handling and ride. All cars have shock absorbers, but some don't have antiroll bars. In fact, it's probable that most drivers don't know whether their car has antiroll bars or what they look like. Fewer still know what they do. For that matter, even though shock absorbers are frequently discussed by car owners, few know what they do. Let's take a closer look at these devices.

WHAT SHOCK ABSORBERS REALLY DO

This heading should be enough to suggest that shock absorbers do something other than what is generally thought. In spite of their name, shock absorbers don't absorb shock. Springs absorb shock. Shock absorbers are devices designed to slow down the rate of shock transfer from the road to the vehicle chassis. When a car goes over a bump, the wheel moves up. Some of the shock of the bump is absorbed by the tire as it flexes, but a large bump or a tire with high air pressure transfers some of the shock to the axle. Then the axle moves up. If the car frame were solidly attached to the axle, the body and frame would move the same amount. Any passengers inside the car would move the same amount. The result would be an uncomfortable ride with the car and passengers bouncing from one bump to the next.

Springs are installed between the axle and the frame to absorb some of the energy of the axle movement. Engineers carefully design the characteristics of the springs to control the amount of energy that the springs absorb. Springs might be designed for a very soft ride in which the wheel and axle can move several inches, or they can be designed for a firm ride with the wheel and axle moving only a small amount. In all cases, springs flex to absorb the energy of the moving wheel and axle.

What happens to that energy that the spring absorbs? It doesn't just disappear. If there were no way for the spring to get rid of the energy it would keep on absorbing more and more until it reached its capacity and broke. Obviously, we don't want that to happen, nor can it happen. Also, the spring is not only attached to the axle; it is attached to the car frame. Figure 4-1 shows a spring partially compressed by a bump. If the spring were not attached to the frame, there would be no resistance to the axle movement and the spring would simply move with it.

Now think back to high school physics class. One thing you learned there was that for every action there is an equal and opposite reaction. In terms of our car and spring, the axle moves and compresses the spring. The spring presses against the car frame. That's one action. The reaction is that the car presses against the spring. The car will move some, depending upon how heavy it is and how stiff the spring is, but the car is pressing back. That forces the spring to release its energy against the wheel and axle. That reaction becomes another action, which becomes another reaction, and so on. If something did not stop the chain of action/reaction, it would continue indefinitely.

One thing that eventually would stop the chain is friction. Some energy is dissipated as friction in each cycle, but the complete loss takes too long. We've all seen the result when we've watched a car with worn-out shock absorbers rocking and rolling down the street.

To dissipate the energy more quickly and give a controlled, safe ride, engineers developed shock absorbers. All the shock absorbers do is slow down the rate of transfer of energy between the axle and the frame. Shock absorbers simply dampen the action. To get an idea of how they work, imagine trying to shove your fist through ten inches of soft mud. The speed of your fist is slowed until there is very little force left by the time you reach the other side. The mud

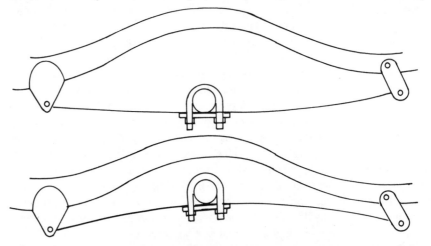

Fig. 4-1. The top drawing shows a spring and chassis section in a normal position. Going over a large bump would deflect the spring to the position shown in the bottom drawing. The energy stored in the compressed spring will cause the body of the car to move upward.

has dampened the action. Shock absorbers dampen the action of axle and body. In some countries, shock absorbers are called dampeners or snubbers.

KINDS OF SHOCK ABSORBERS

Some of the earliest shock absorbers were just friction devices. Two plates faced with material similar to brake lining were held tightly together. One was attached to the axle and the other to the frame through levers. As the axle moved, the two plates were forced to move against each other. The resulting friction dampened the action.

Along with technical development of other automobile systems, new ways evolved to dampen axle movement. The most promising method, the hydraulic shock absorber, is used in several variations on today's vehicles. This device, in its simplest form, is simply a cylinder fitted with a piston. One end of the cylinder is fastened to the frame, and the piston is fastened to the axle. A small opening, or valve, is placed in the piston head. The cylinder is filled with fluid, which is forced through the valve as the axle moves the piston. Because the fluid can only move through the valve very slowly, the system works as a movement dampening device. By varying the sizes of the cylinder, piston, and valve, engineers can control the dampening action to get the characteristics they want. This is the type of shock absorber found on most cars.

In response to increasing car speeds and demands of car owners, shock absorbers have been designed for specific types of service. Original equipment (OEM) shock absorbers are satisfactory for most drivers, but there are always a few who demand a better ride or longer life. Some drivers, such as you, believe that better shock absorbers can give better control and safety.

One response to these demands is the so-called heavy-duty shock absorber. These usually are made much like OEM shocks but with larger diameter cylinder and pistons. The sales people like to talk about special valving, but size is the main difference. That's not to denigrate heavy-duty shocks. They will usually give better control and last much longer than OEM shocks.

The recent rise in popularity of off-road racing has resulted in a major modification of the hydraulic shock absorber. Off-road racers quickly found that there was a problem with even heavy-duty shocks. When the fluid in the shock is forced through the valve, two things happen. First, heat is generated, causing the fluid to expand and reducing the dampening action. Second, the fluid tends to foam. The more bumps the vehicle takes, the more action the shock absorber is required to handle, and the more foam is produced. Foam is comprised of tiny droplets of fluid mixed with air. Foam goes through the valve much more easily than does fluid. When any significant amount of foam is produced within the shock, the dampening action becomes unpredictable or nonexistent. Control of the vehicle is degraded, and safety decreases.

To control the foaming action, engineers have added a compressed gas, usually nitrogen. The nitrogen displaces air from the cylinder and reduces foaming. The result is a more controlled ride under heavy-duty conditions. Most drivers will be satisfied with the action of heavy-duty shocks. Those drivers seeking the best control available will likely choose gas-charged shocks. Figure 4-2 shows the basic OEM shock compared with one that is gas-charged.

Contrary to popular belief, shock absorbers are not intended to carry weight. Their design makes it impossible. In spite of that, many owners talk about their shocks as weak and as not carrying the load. They "prove" it by pointing out that the back or front of their car sags. What is really happening is that the springs are not doing their job. The springs might be worn, or the owner might be simply overloading them. There are dangers in overloading the suspension system of any vehicle. The axles, wheels, springs, and tires all were selected for a specific weight range. Each component was engineered to carry an amount of weight safely. Adding more than that weight develops an unsafe condition.

There will always be some owners who try to carry more weight in their vehicle than it was designed to carry. Shock absorber engineers have developed two types of shocks to help them in their dangerous mission. One weight-carrying shock absorber uses a light coil spring around the exterior of the cylinder to carry some of the vehicle weight. The other type has an air reservoir inside the cylinder that can be pressurized. The compressed air acts as an additional spring. Both types are popular with drivers who find themselves frequently carrying enough weight in the trunk or cargo area to make the rear of the vehicle sag. I don't recommend either type because both are intended to work with a dangerously overloaded condition that should not be encouraged.

There is another type of shock that uses a compressed air reservoir in a different manner. This is the air-adjustable shock. Air pressure is used to adjust the stiffness or firmness of the shock, not to carry part of the load. Varying the air pressure is used to tailor the ride characteristics. For example, if the family is going for an afternoon drive and a gentle ride is wanted, air pressure can be very light. If you are driving by yourself and want firmer control, you can increase the air pressure.

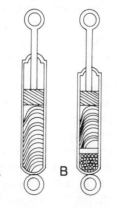

Fig. 4-2. An OEM shock absorber (A) is subject to foaming of the hydraulic fluid which degrades the dampening action. A charge of nitrogen in the gas-charged shock (B) adds sufficient pressure to reduce foaming.

WHICH SHOCK AND HOW MANY

Every vehicle eventually reaches a point where the shocks are sufficiently worn that they no longer perform adequately. That point is usually reached long before the driver is aware of it. The change in performance is so gradual that loss of shock dampening has occurred without being noticed. Tire wear patterns become abnormal. The ride has deteriorated in subtle ways. Vehicle control isn't quite as good as it used to be. The problem is that by the time these factors become obvious, damage has been done.

You should examine shock absorbers every 5,000 miles to see if they are still doing their job. Check the piston rod where it works in and out of the seal. The rod should be shiny and smooth. Any pits or other corrosion are a sign that the seal will soon be leaking fluid. A visible fluid leak, of course, is an additional indication that the shock should be replaced.

If the shocks pass the visual inspection, press down on the bumper hard enough to deflect it at least a couple of inches, and quickly remove your weight. The bumper should rise, drop a bit, and return to its original position. If it continues to rise and drop more than two cycles, the shocks need to be replaced.

Which shocks should you buy? Is it really necessary to buy the highest-priced ones? In selecting any replacement component, you need to consider the question of cost vs. service. OEM shocks are inexpensive. Heavy-duty shocks cost about twice as much. Gas-charged shocks might cost three times as much as OEM models. There are others that cost even more. To answer the cost/service question you have to know how long each can be expected to last. The average life for OEM shocks is about 20,000 miles. Some drivers will ruin a pair in 5,000 miles. Others might stretch shock life to as much as 30,000 miles. The difference is mainly in how the car is driven. Hitting lots of potholes and bumps will wear shocks out faster.

Heavy-duty shocks can be expected to last much longer. To give an illustration, at 110,000 miles I replaced the heavy-duty shocks that came on the front of my van when it was purchased. With over 130,000 miles the rear shocks still give no indication that they need to be replaced. Much of the mileage has been accumulated while the vehicle was towing a travel trailer. Is 110,000 miles unusual? I doubt it. I have always made it a practice to get a new vehicle with heavy-duty shocks. I don't remember ever replacing them with less than 70,000 miles of service. Is probable service of three to four times the miles worth twice the price? I think so. In addition, heavy-duty shocks give better control over their lifetime.

In spite of that experience, when it comes time for replacement, I don't put on heavy-duty shocks. I buy and recommend the gas-charged variety. They might not last any longer, but I believe they will give better control for at least as long as the heavy-duty shocks. I like that peace of mind.

Recently it has become quite common to see vehicles with two, three, even four shock absorbers at each wheel. Why? There are only two reasons for using more than one shock per wheel. The first has to do with appearance. Some owners of light trucks and utility vehicles believe that multiple shocks add to their vehicle's appearance. Since the truck is theirs, I can't say that they are wrong, but I do know that multiple shocks can give a ride that is only slightly better than having no springs at all. Having too many shocks dampens the action to the point that there is no action.

The second reason for multiple shocks is that many owners replace their tires and wheels with much larger ones. The result might be a tire and wheel weighing twice what the original ones did. The original shocks were not designed to handle the energy of that additional weight. More shock-dampening power is needed. If you drastically change the size of your wheels and tires, you might have to add multiple shocks. How many? There are no engineering data, but it seems logical to use two shocks per wheel when the new wheels and tires weigh twice as much as the original ones.

INSTALLING SHOCK ABSORBERS

Suppose your shocks are showing signs of imminent demise, or you want to improve handling and ride by installing better shocks. The question is, do you install them yourself or have someone else do it for you?

The answer depends upon several factors. First, does your car have Mac-Pherson struts or separate springs and shocks? MacPherson struts are found in the front suspensions of most cars built since about 1980. MacPherson struts are an assembly containing several parts, but shocks and springs are the main ones. You can replace the shocks without replacing the springs, but for shock replacement you still have to dismount the entire assembly. The job requires special tools and, if not done correctly, can be dangerous. Unless you are an above average mechanic and have the special tools, I recommend you leave MacPherson strut repair to your friendly mechanic.

Older cars and most vans and trucks use separate shocks and springs, all of them on all four wheels. Many newer cars also use separate assemblies on the rear wheels. Replacement of shocks on most of these vehicles is relatively simple. The biggest hazard is likely to be severely rusted threads on the nuts and bolts holding everything together. The threads on older vehicles, especially in areas that use lots of salt on the roads in winter, can be so badly rusted that removal requires using a torch or power wrench. Inspection of the bolts can give you a clue as to what to expect. If the external surfaces of the nuts and bolts show only moderate rust, you can probably remove them with hand tools.

Tools needed include socket wrenches, jack, hammer, and stands. The stands are used to support the vehicle frame while you crawl under. *Never under any circumstances crawl under a vehicle not supported by stands*. The next person who has a car fall off a jack onto him will not be the first one. Trying to support the corner of a car on your chest, head, or leg is no fun. Before crawling under any vehicle, make absolutely certain it is solidly supported by adequate stands and cannot roll off.

Each vehicle is an individual case. If you have any doubts at all about the process on your vehicle, find the proper repair manual and study it carefully. Manuals for nearly any automobile or light truck can be purchased at most book stores. Some auto parts stores have repair manuals for popular cars. Many parts stores and nearly all libraries have manuals on reserve or to be checked out. Study them.

Although specifics will vary, there is one general process for replacement of shocks. Securely block the wheels that will not be raised. Jack up the wheels where shocks will be replaced and place solid supports under the frame. The wheel and associated suspension parts will need to hang free. Remove both wheels. (Shocks are always replaced in pairs.) Remove the nuts that hold each end of shock. Note the arrangement of washers and other small parts. Drive out the bolt at the lower end. Some upper ends will also have a bolt that needs to be driven out. Remove the shock and rubber insulators. Install new insulators. Install the upper end of shock and insert the bolt (and washers) if one is used. Push up firmly on the lower end of shock until it can be placed in its bracket. Insert the bolt and washers. Tighten all nuts to the torque specifications given. Install the wheels. Remove the stands. You're finished.

WHY YOU NEED ANTIROLL BARS

When a vehicle goes around a corner at any speed faster than a walk, there are lots of forces at work. Centrifugal force, the force that pulls objects away from the center of a turn, is one. Among other results, centrifugal force makes the car body lean toward the outside of the turn. The faster and sharper the corner, the greater the lean. Lean can be severe enough to lift one of the inside wheels or it can cause the car to roll over. It's best to keep all four wheels on the pavement. Rolling the car over can mess up the paint and make you look foolish.

Antiroll bars are used to control the body lean. Figure 4-3 shows some of the forces at work when the body leans and how an antiroll bar transfers these forces. The effect is to reduce body roll to some degree and to reduce weight transfer on the wheels at the other end of the car.

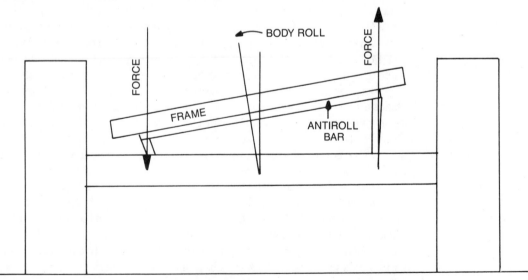

Fig. 4-3. As the car goes around a right turn, the body tends to lean to the left. The antiroll bar is pressed down on the left. The pressure is transferred back to the right wheel, pressing it down.

Most rear-wheel-drive cars come from the factory with antiroll bars installed in the front end, but they are the usual compromise for average conditions. Remember, manufacturers are more concerned with building a car with a soft ride than one with crisp handling. In most instances, handling can be improved by careful selection of an antiroll bar. Installing a stiffer antiroll bar at the front end will decrease body roll and delay loss of traction at the inside rear wheel. In most cases, that will give an improvement in handling. However, if carried to extremes, excessive understeer and lifting of the inside front wheel might result.

Unfortunately, it is impossible to predict accurately the steering characteristics that will result from installing a stiffer front antiroll bar. On a car with independent suspension at both front and rear, the result is likely to be an increase in understeer. On a car with independent front suspension and a solid rear axle, the result of stiffening the front antiroll bar is likely to be a decrease in understeer. Keeping those tendencies in mind, your best approach is to make a careful trial.

Most rear-wheel-drive cars will not have an antiroll bar installed on the rear suspension. Adding one or stiffening an existing bar is likely to create oversteer. Earlier I stated that oversteer is usually undesirable, but there are some situations where it might be wanted. For example, if you are going to drive in slalom races, you might want oversteer to help negotiate the very sharp turns. Typically, a car will understeer in very sharp turns. Increasing oversteer by installing a rear antiroll bar might be just the factor needed for slalom races, but be very careful driving such a car on the street. Oversteer tends to become more extreme at high speeds. A car set up for slalom racing can be dangerous on the highway. A compromise might be to install the antiroll bar but leave one end disconnected except for racing.

Front-wheel-drive cars have the antiroll bar at the rear because it is desirable to increase traction for the front driving wheels. Increasing roll stiffness at the rear accomplishes that. Adding roll stiffness at the rear of front-wheel-drive cars also decreases the understeer that seems to plague most of them. Installing an antiroll bar at the front of front-wheel-drive cars is usually undesirable because it tends to aggravate the existing understeer condition. The only exception is when a rear wheel tends to lift during steady turns. Approach the cure carefully.

Because antiroll bars exert no force unless the body rolls or one wheel lifts more than the other, they cause no increase in ride stiffness. However, when only one wheel hits a bump and rises, the antiroll bar is twisted as if the body had leaned. The result is a momentary increase in ride stiffness. The increase will not be nearly as severe as if you use stiffer springs. A combination that most drivers find desirable is to use the relatively soft springs that the car comes equipped with and a somewhat stiffer antiroll bar to control body lean and improve cornering.

Installing an antiroll bar is usually easy. Most are available with brackets that make installation a simple, bolt-on job. Selecting the proper bar is not so easy. Arrange for a trial installation, if possible. Start with a bar slightly stiffer than the one already in place. Drive the car and see how it handles. If you have a sedan, an antiroll bar from a station wagon of the same make and model will be an inexpensive purchase.

TRACTION BARS

Traction bars are another device sometimes used on rear-wheel-drive vehicles. They are very popular with drag racers or drivers who want to look like drag racers. As Fig. 4-4 shows, heavy acceleration tends to twist the rear axle and springs. The result is rapid loading and unloading of the springs, causing the rear wheels intermittently to lose traction and hop. Severe wheel hop can cause uncomfortable vibration and breakage of suspension parts.

Figure 4-5 shows one type of traction bar. There are several others available. All are designed to resist rear spring wind-up during heavy acceleration and reduce wheel hop. Most also raise the rear of the car and increase the stiffness of the rear suspension.

Do you need a traction bar? As stated above, they are only used by drag racers and drivers who want to look like drag racers. Unless you fit into one of those groups, there is probably no good reason to install a traction bar. An exception would be a lightweight car with lots of power. With such a car, maintaining traction on the driving wheels can be a problem. A traction bar may be desirable under these conditions. Stiffening the rear suspension by installing a traction bar can significantly reduce the wheel spin associated with high power and low weight.

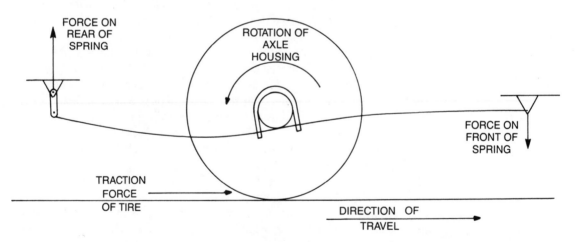

Fig. 4-4. Heavy acceleration tends to twist the rear axle, causing the springs to load up. The spring will then release its energy, causing the wheels to hop.

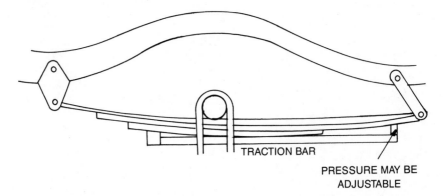

TRACTION BAR

PRESSURE MAY BE
ADJUSTABLE

Fig. 4-5. A traction bar resists rear axle twist and spring loading. The amount of resistance is usually adjustable.

5
CHAPTER

To Lift or Not to Lift

FOR THE PAST FEW YEARS SOME RATHER STRANGE LOOKING VEHICLES HAVE
been part of the traffic scene. Light trucks and utility vehicles with bodies high
above their normal location abound. I have seen some that required either gym-
nastics or a short step ladder to gain the driver's seat.

REASONS FOR LIFTING

Since it can be assumed that building a vehicle with the body several inches
above its normal location must cost a sizable amount of money, there must be a
reason for doing so. Actually, there are several reasons.

Several years ago a monster truck called Bigfoot appeared on the scene.
Pictures of Bigfoot were printed in most of the magazines in any way related to
light trucks and utility vehicles. Bigfoot was shown at fairs and rallies and auto
shows across the country. Perhaps the trend toward lifted vehicles did not start
with Bigfoot, but the beast surely did exert a large influence on the genre.

Other monsters followed, with the owner of each trying to outlift the others. Subframes were built from military vehicle components, farm tractor tires
were fitted, supercharged engines installed, and outlandish names given. Building and showing monster trucks, as they became known, was suddenly big business with the trucks costing tens of thousands of dollars. A peripheral sport,
junker smashing, developed. The object was to see how many old cars the monster could smash by running over them. One recent entry in the smashed-car
derby uses the undercarriage and tracks from a military tank with a truck body
mounted high above.

Show trucks and cars of one form or another have been popular for decades. Each generation of car/truck owners tries to come up with an idea that hasn't been used before or at least not for a long time. Monster trucks seem to be the present generation's bid for immortality.

Actually, there are at least three groups of reasons for lifting trucks. One, Bigfoot and its emulators, has been mentioned. Even before Bigfoot there was another group with a legitimate interest in getting the bodies of their trucks a bit higher off the ground. These were the off-road drivers. Some off-road drivers were off the road because that was the way they lived or earned their money. They were ranchers, miners, geologists, prospectors, sportsmen, and other whose activities took them off the pavement. Because they frequently had a need to navigate through mud, shallow water, snow, and between large rocks, they needed additional clearance for the tender underparts of their vehicles. Getting stuck in a snowdrift or hung up on a boulder 50 miles from the nearest telephone can make you miss an important appointment.

These owners installed oversize wheels and tires to gain a few inches of "road" clearance. When the larger tires interfered with such body parts as fenders, the offending parts were often cut away. Some owners went a bit further and found ways to lift the body a few inches above the chassis to gain room for larger tires. Lifting the vehicle's body also gained some clearance for running between large boulders. When one of these vehicles accidentally was found in town, the local would-be prospectors and sportsmen were excited with the prospect of a new way of declaring their special identity. Drive a lifted truck and everyone will instantly know that you're a prospector—or something.

Ask one of these drugstore prospectors why he built a truck like that and he'll start telling you about the clearance he has in mud and snow, the back roads and trails he can run, and how he can slip between boulders the size of small houses. Words like "Rubicon" and "Baja" pop up in his conversation. Look more closely and you will see that the only battle scars his truck has come from the same doors that get your car in the local parking lot. Very few of these off-road specialists get farther from home than the local supermarket.

So why the lift? There are two main reasons, one being cosmetic and the other psychological. Many car and truck owners want to be part of the latest fad. If their car isn't raised in the rear or their truck isn't lifted, they feel left out. These owners get a psychological lift from giving their trucks a lift. They identify with the latest car craze or with the few bona fide prospectors and sportsmen. Driving a truck with an extreme amount of lift just intensifies the psychological boost. In another generation these drivers would have been the ones whose cars were lowered until the door sills scraped the pavement.

Another group of owners truly believe that lifted trucks are beautiful. They wouldn't know a boulder from a butte and don't care. They make no pretense of being anything other than what they are, aficionados of lifted trucks. They chrome differential cases and paint axles. A spot of dust or speck of mud would never have the effrontery to land on their truck.

Are these two groups wrong? Of course not. Americans are maintaining a century-old love affair with their cars and trucks. One man's (or woman's) fancy is another's junk. That's the American way.

But what of the driver who really does want to hit the trails? How much lift does he really need? What are the costs in terms of handling and performance?

The latter will be discussed later. Let's deal with how much lift is enough first. In most vehicles, the part nearest the pavement—or rock—is either the differential case or the front axle. As most trucks leave the factory, that clearance is about eight inches, which means that any rock less than eight inches high is no problem. It also means that snow less than eight inches deep will be touched by nothing other than the tires. Snow or mud deeper than eight inches does strike the front or rear axle. So does a rock higher than eight inches. Neither gets anywhere near the body because the body is higher.

The stock tires on most light trucks and utility vehicles have a radius of about 14 inches. Installing 31-inch tires, about the maximum before lifting the body is necessary, gives a radius of 15½ inches, an additional 1½ inches of clearance. That's not much, but it might be critical if the rock in the middle of the road is nine inches high. Installing 35-inch tires, popular with the would-be prospectors, gives 3½ more inches of clearance than stock tires, but requires some sort of frame lift. Adding these large tires also causes lots of other problems which we will get to shortly. The question still is, "How much clearance is really needed?" A related question is, "How much are you willing to pay for the additional clearance?" Money, though important, is not the only cost.

CENTER OF GRAVITY AFFECTS HANDLING

One of the big changes when larger tires are installed is that the center of gravity is raised. As long as the vehicle is going in a straight line, it makes little difference where the center of gravity is located. When you start to turn, either to go around a corner or to avoid another car, the location of the center of gravity becomes critical. A rule of engineering is that the higher the center of gravity, the greater the body roll. We have previously discussed the problems with body roll. With high center of gravity, cornering becomes less precise and emergency maneuvers become more difficult and less controlled. Under severe conditions, the vehicle will simply roll over much more easily. The necessity to keep cornering precise and maintain traction is a large reason why race cars are built as low to the pavement as possible.

In any braking situation there is some weight transfer to the front wheels. Weight and traction on the rear wheels become less. The greater the weight transfer, the less weight there is on the rear wheels. A frequently encountered result is that the rear end of the vehicle becomes so light that the wheels lose traction and the car swaps ends. Raising the center of gravity aggravates the situation.

Fig. 5-1. Lifting a truck, such as this one, raises the center of gravity. Handling is impaired.

Raising the center of gravity by three or four inches might not seem like much. After all, the vehicle might be at least 60 inches high. What is forgotten is that the center of gravity on a vehicle stock from the factory may be only 12 inches above the pavement. Raising it another four inches represents a 33⅓ percent increase in height for the center of gravity. That is extreme.

OTHER NEGATIVE RESULTS FROM LIFTING

Getting the torque from the rear of the transmission to the differential is the job of the driveshaft. Because the rear wheels are continually moving up and down in reference to the body, universal joints are placed in the driveshaft. These permit the torque to turn small corners. In effect, universal joints are rotating hinges in the driveshaft. Universal joints work fine as long as they are not required to bend more than a few degrees and the angle is exactly the same at both ends of the driveshaft. Because the driveshafts on light trucks and utility vehicles are relatively short, lifting the frame can cause the universal joint angles to become excessive. Vibration results and the universal joints don't last very long.

Some builders have tried rotating the rear axle slightly to reduce the angle. This introduces a difference in the angularity between the joints at either end of the driveshaft and does not reduce the problem. There seems to be no solution to driveshaft problems with lift of more than about three inches. Even that much reduces universal joint life.

Another negative to excessive lift is the matter of getting into the vehicle. Getting out is no problem; you just slide out and down. The effect is not graceful and can be slightly hazardous under some conditions—an icy landing area, for example—but that seems not to bother most owners. Climbing up can be more difficult. Utility vehicles and light trucks are slightly higher than cars to start with. Add the excessive lift that some owners want, and entry becomes a gymnastic event. Skirts are definitely not advised. In some instances, a short ladder would be a real asset.

None of us expects to be involved in an accident, but the papers continually remind us that accidents do happen. An accident involving a vehicle with excessive lift, anything over two inches, can be more than slightly exciting. Bumpers might not absorb the effects of any major interaction between vehicles, but they do mitigate the damage a bit. If one of the vehicles has been lifted more than a couple of inches, the bumpers might as well not be there. A lifted vehicle attacking another from the rear is going to climb right into the front vehicle's trunk and passenger space. The frame of the front vehicle will have no opportunity to absorb any of the impact. In such an accident, it is very easy for the gasoline tank of the front vehicle to be crushed. The result is messy.

On the other hand, if the front vehicle should happen to be lifted, the rear vehicle is going to go under and into the lifted vehicle's fuel tank. Again, the results are messy.

Engineers spend a lot of time designing crash safety into vehicles. Frames and bodies are designed to absorb impact in a manner that will preserve the integrity of the passenger space as much as possible. When modifiers change a vehicle by lifting or lowering it, they destroy the efforts of the safety engineers. The results are unpredictable.

LIFTING, BIG TIRES, AND GEARING

There is also the problem of gearing. The question and answer columns of four-wheel drive magazines are full of letters from owners who complain that their vehicles have no power now. "All I did was put on 37-inch tires and lift the frame to clear the tires. Now my truck won't get out of its own way. What can I do?"

Assume that the truck came with a gear ratio of 3.25 to 1, a common gear ratio these days. Assume that it originally wore 28-inch tires. At 55 mph the engine turned 2,145 revolutions per minute (rpm). Most engines in light trucks and utility vehicles develop their best torque and fuel mileage at about 2,500 rpm. At 2,145 rpm our hypothetical truck has marginal torque. Replace the tires with 37 inchers and at 55 mph the engine is turning only 1,625 rpm. That's only slightly above idle. The engine has no chance to develop either torque or horsepower. It's no wonder the owner says it "won't get out of its own way."

What's to be done? To get that truck back to where its engine is turning fast enough to develop the torque needed for good performance, you need to change the truck's gears to about 5.00 to 1. That's a drastic change and might not be possible in some vehicles. Further, remember that the gears will have to be changed in both axles. That's expensive.

Finally, there will eventually come a time when you wish to get rid of your vehicle. Selling or trading a truck or utility vehicle that has been lifted immediately raises alarms in the mind of the person evaluating the vehicle. Has it been abused by much driving off the pavement? Has the frame been bent by operation on rough ground? The universal joints are almost certainly badly worn. What else has the owner done that might not be apparent? Unless you are lucky enough to find a buyer who is either ignorant of these possibilities or who simply dismisses his better judgment, you can expect to be offered a lower price for your vehicle than if it had not been lifted.

None of what I have just written will deter the owner who is intent on joining the would-be-prospector set or who simply wants the most outlandish truck on the lot. There are many who will argue with my position. To all of you I would simply suggest that if you think the real prospectors and back country sportsmen need lifted trucks, you take a look. Find a grizzled prospector or hunting guide and look at his truck. The odds are high that it won't be lifted an inch.

6
CHAPTER

Tires and Wheels for Handling

LOTS OF MONEY IS SPENT ON GETTING A POWERFUL, HIGH PERFORMANCE ENGINE. More is spent on tuning the car's suspension. Big bucks are spent on body work and a fancy paint job. But, when it comes to spending money on the point where all the rest hits the road, owners seem to lose interest. It seems that what they want is a set of flashy wheels and tires with a large, white imprint on the sidewalls. There is much more to selection of tires and wheels than that.

TIRE SIZES AND TYPES AND THEIR EFFECT

For many years all tires were bias-ply construction. Bias-ply tires get their name from the fact that the plies crisscross at an angle, usually between 32 and 40 degrees, with the center line of the tire. The ply material might be any of several different fabrics. Cotton was used for many years but gave way to such synthetics as rayon, nylon, and others. Cotton tended to rot and quit unexpectedly. Synthetics greatly improved the life of bias-ply tires. There is nothing wrong with bias-ply tires for average use. They are the least expensive of all tires and are available in a wide range of sizes.

For severe conditions bias-ply tires do have some disadvantages. For example, they squirm where they contact the road. The tire tread actually moves as the weight of the vehicle compresses it against the pavement. The squirm increases tire wear and can give a sort of uneasy feeling to the handling of the vehicle.

To overcome tire squirm, tire manufacturers added a belt around the circumference of the tire just under the tread. Belts are made of steel, fiberglass, and various synthetic fibers. Belted bias-ply tires are a great improvement. Most of the squirm is gone. Tread life is improved and the strength of the tire is increased. But belted bias-ply tires tend to have a rather harsh ride. Manufacturers countered the harshness by capitalizing on the increased strength. They were able to cut the number of plies in half because of the strength of the belt. The result was a tire that rode better and lasted longer. Belted bias-ply tires are still popular because they are relatively inexpensive.

Shortly after belted bias-ply tires were introduced, another style of tire, radial-ply, hit the market. On radial-ply tires the plies run from bead to bead, crossing the center line of the tire at 90 degrees. This makes a very soft-running but rather weak tire. To add strength, designers gave radial-ply tires a multi-ply belt made of steel, fiberglass, or a synthetic fiber. The result is a tire that conforms well to the pavement, has a larger ''footprint'' than bias-ply tires, wears well, and has low rolling resistance. In almost every area, radial-ply tires are superior to any other type. They are somewhat more expensive, but the additional tread life more than compensates for the additional cost. Figure 6-1 shows the differences in construction among the three types of tires.

Radial tires react to turning and braking forces much more quickly than bias tires because they are more flexible and grip the road better. As a result, it is dangerous to mix the two types on a car; handling behavior can be unpredictable. If the two types must be mixed for a short time—with use of a bias spare, for example—be sure the bias tire goes on the front of the car. Driving with the mix should be slow and careful.

Sidewalls of radial tires are more flexible than bias tires. This flexibility keeps more tread of the radial tire on the pavement. Figure 6-2 shows the effect of the two types in a corner. Radial steering seems quicker and more responsive. An additional benefit is that steering is much less affected when you're crossing a ridge in the road or when you're driving a road that has grooves worn in from the traffic of heavy trucks. Bias tires tend to follow the high edges of the ridges or grooves, and they give a very uncomfortable ride. The car is contin-

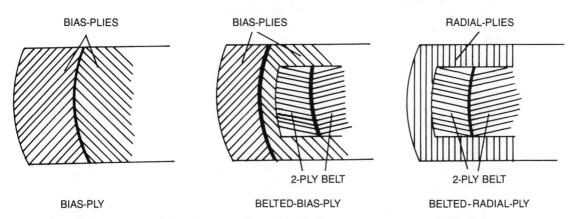

BIAS-PLIES BIAS-PLIES RADIAL-PLIES

2-PLY BELT 2-PLY BELT

BIAS-PLY BELTED-BIAS-PLY BELTED-RADIAL-PLY

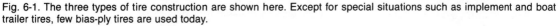

Fig. 6-1. The three types of tire construction are shown here. Except for special situations such as implement and boat trailer tires, few bias-ply tires are used today.

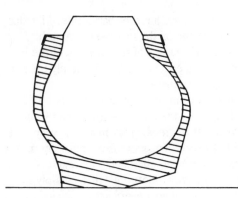

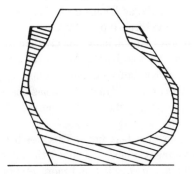

Fig. 6-2. The different responses of bias-ply and radial-ply tires in cornering are shown here. The radial-ply tire has much better cornering ability.

ually moving from side to side, following the ridge, and requires continual correction. A car equipped with radial tires is very little affected by such ridges and grooves.

Response to crosswinds will vary according to car design and type of tire. I once had a Volkswagen ''Bug'' that was uncomfortable to drive in crosswinds because it needed continual correction. Every gust moved the car sideways. After I installed a set of radial tires, the problem almost totally disappeared. It was like driving a different car.

Radial tires sometimes give a slightly harsher ride at low speeds and might be a bit noisier. These are minor problems and might not be noticeable. Because of their decreased rolling resistance, radial tires will usually give a noticeable increase in fuel mileage and top speed.

All of these factors make the radial tire the most desirable for improved handling and performance. Simply replacing bias tires with radials might give a 5 percent improvement in fuel mileage. Radials will certainly give improved tread life and superior handling. Car manufacturers agree. Most cars come from the factory with radials.

Radial tires do impose more severe loads on wheels than do bias tires. Installing radial tires on some older vehicles with wheels designed for bias tires can result in failure of the wheels. This has been most prevalent among some older, heavy vehicles such as motorhomes and light trucks, and it's a factor worth considering if you are thinking of installing radials on an older vehicle. The dealer for your make of car should be able to tell you if the change is safe.

TREAD TYPES

Looking at the various tread types in a tire store can be confusing. It seems that each manufacturer must have at least a dozen different tread styles at a time. You almost get the idea that tire manufacturers change styles of tread as often as dress designers change women's fashions. You're not wrong. Follow the designs of any manufacturer for a few years and you will see continual change. After a couple of years, try and buy a mate for that new spare that was never placed on the ground, and you will find the style has been discontinued. Was something wrong with the design? Not necessarily. If you could check that company's catalog for several past years, you would very likely find that today's patterns are very similar, if not identical, to those of past years.

Over a period of time, there are changes in tire treads, but they are usually very small. Not too noticeable, but very important, are changes made in tread designs of snow tires and all-weather patterns. These coarse patterns used to be very noisy. Using data processed by computers, designers came up with new patterns that are effective on slick pavement and in snow or mud without being excessively noisy.

One recent new/old tire design is the all-season tread. This tread design is an attempt to combine the characteristics of snow treads with less aggressive treads made for summer use. The same thing was done back in the 1940s by Goodyear, among others. Goodyear called theirs the all-weather tread.

Snow tires became very popular in the northern tier of states several years ago. Tires designed with less aggressive treads for warm weather didn't work well on ice and snow. Snow tended to clog the finer tread openings in ordinary tires, making them lose traction. One answer was a more open, coarse tread. These greatly improved traction on ice and snow but were noisy on dry pavement. They also tended to wear faster on dry pavement than did ordinary treads. But drivers objected to the necessity to have two sets of tires, one set for winter use and another for warmer weather. Tire manufacturers responded with the all-season tread design. The new treads were nearly as open and coarse as snow treads, but because of the implementation of information learned from computer studies of tire treads, they were much quieter. Tread life was also significantly improved over snow tires. Today, all-season tread designs are very commonly used on cars in the northern part of the country year-round. Figure 6-3 shows examples of ordinary treads and all-season treads.

The use of small grooves, or sipes, across the tread surface is another example of the use of computer data in designing a tire tread. As highway speeds increased, vehicles began hydroplaning on wet pavement. Hydroplaning occurs when water caught between the tire tread and the pavement cannot escape. The entrapped water becomes a film holding the tire above the pavement. Without contact with the pavement, the tire has no traction. The effect is

Fig. 6-3. The more open tread of the all-season tire on the left gives better traction in snow and on ice or wet pavement than does the standard tread.

very much like driving on ice. Computer data showed that cutting small grooves across the tread would permit the water to escape and let the tread maintain contact with the pavement. Although hydroplaning might still occur at very high speeds in heavy rain, the risk at more normal speeds has greatly diminished.

ASPECT RATIO OF TIRES

For many years, aspect ratio of tires was a nonterm. It didn't exist. A 6.50 × 16 tire was a tire with a cross-section of 6.5 inches fitted on a rim with a diameter of 16 inches. If you had cut through one of those tires from tread to bead, the section would have been nearly circular. The distance from the rim to the tread, casing height, was equal to the distance from side to side at the widest point, cross-section. Aspect ratio would have been 100 percent. Things are different now. Seldom are casing height and cross-section the same. Aspect ratio, the relationship between the casing height and cross-section, has become an important term. Aspect ratios of tires now range from 85 percent down to 50 percent or lower. Tires with low aspect ratios are sometimes called low-profile tires. Figure 6-4 shows tires with different aspect ratios all designed for the same diameter wheel. In general, tires with low aspect ratios give better cornering and would be selected for high performance driving.

There are several things to consider when you select a low-profile tire. Usually, a low-profile tire requires a wider rim than a normal tire of the same

Fig. 6-4. Tires of different aspect ratios are shown here. The series 50 tire is wider and lower than the series 60 and 70 tires. The wider tread gives better cornering ability.

nominal size. Tire dealers have charts showing the size rim required by each tire size. Putting a tire on a wheel that is too narrow or too wide causes both the sidewalls and tread to distort. The result can be shortened tread life. In extreme cases, the tire can be forced from the rim, losing air rapidly as if the tire had blown out. Tires and wheels must be properly matched in size for both safety and performance.

Another effect of changing tire sizes relates to clearance. Original size tires and wheels are selected to maintain clearance between the tire and all parts of the chassis. Using a tire with a wider cross-section might reduce clearance to the point that the tire rubs against the fender or frame. The result can be destruction of the tire and a serious accident. Before buying low-profile tires, be certain that there is ample clearance between the tire and all parts of the frame and body. Remember that going over a bump reduces vertical clearance. Remember, too, that bumps sometimes occur when the front wheels are turned sharply.

Tire size also affects gearing. The effect of installing large tires and wheels was discussed earlier, but it bears some repetition here. Many drivers buy a set of radical, low-profile tires and wonder what happened to their mileage. It's true that they also suddenly realized an increase in apparent power. What happened?

Going to a low-profile tire decreases the diameter of the tire. The tire moves a shorter distance with each revolution. How much shorter? Well, going from a P235/85 to a P235/50 might change the diameter from 29 inches to 26.5 inches in one popular brand of tire. That's a decrease of 8.6 percent. If your car had 3.25 rear end gears, making that tire change would be the same as installing 3.50 gears. Speedometer readings would be 8.6 percent low both in distance and in speed. Engine speeds would have to increase by 8.6 percent to maintain the same road speed. Theoretically, acceleration would increase by 8.6 percent. (But read the fine print.) Actual acceleration would increase by only the square root of 8.6 percent—less than 3 percent. Top speed would be reduced by an unknown amount. Lots of trade-offs.

If you are willing and able to find a larger wheel you may be able to find a low-profile tire that has nearly the same diameter as your original equipment tire and wheel. Tire and wheel dealers have charts that give diameters. Check with them.

One more factor to consider is the carrying capacity of your new tires. Decreasing the aspect ratio might reduce the amount of air the tire holds. Tire carrying capacity is based on air capacity. The tires you select must have ample capacity to carry the car and its contents—you, your family, and whatever you take with you—safely. Anything less is dangerous.

WHEELS FOR LOOKS AND HANDLING

One of the first things many car owners buy is a set of custom wheels. Look in any performance shop, and wheels are very prominently displayed. The car look of today is definitely "wheels."

The proper selection of wheel size and type can affect performance and handling. Most owners want wider wheels in the belief that wider wheels and tires mean increased traction. Increased width can give greater traction, but under some conditions the opposite is true. Wet pavement, for example, can cause wide tires to hydroplane at a lower speed than narrow tires. To some degree, the same is true when you drive on snow. Wide tires spread the weight over a wider area, giving less weight per square inch of contact surface. More compromises.

Wider wheels and tires are also frequently heavier. Adding weight to wheels and tires increases the unsprung weight of the vehicle and usually causes the ride comfort to deteriorate. Heavy wheels and tires also increase rolling resistance. This can decrease acceleration and increase stopping distance.

These are some of the factors you have to consider when you select custom wheels. The problem of clearance has previously been raised. One partial solution to the clearance problem is to increase the offset of the wheel. Ideally, the hub of a wheel where it attaches to the axle should be directly under the center of the rim. That's the way most OEM wheels are built. Because of wide tires, some wheels are built with positive offset. In effect, the rim is moved toward the outside, away from the vertical line of the mounting surface. Figure 6-5 shows a wheel with positive offset.

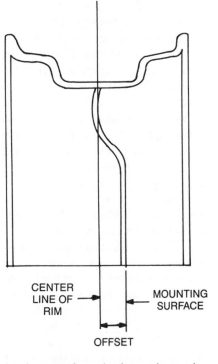

Fig. 6-5. Positive offset in a wheel means that the centerline of the wheel is moved away from the mounting surface toward the outside of the car.

CENTER LINE OF RIM

MOUNTING SURFACE

OFFSET

A wheel with positive offset moves the tire away from the frame, increasing the clearance. By the same measure, it moves the tire closer to the outside fender edge, decreasing the clearance. Using wide tires on wheels with positive offset usually requires some trimming of the fenders for clearance. Most states also require the addition of fender flairs to control water and debris thrown from the tires.

Life seems so full of compromises. That is especially true when you start to modify an existing object, such as a car. By moving the tire farther away from the frame when you use a wheel with positive offset, you also increase the loads on axle bearings and steering gear. This makes the car steer harder. Extra toe-in might be required to keep steering loads at a safe level. If you could carefully analyze all the changes in loads, you would come to the realization that it is best to keep the offset on front wheels as near stock as possible. The possible gains aren't worth the probable losses.

The same is true with the rear wheels. Steering loads don't become a problem, but bearing loads do increase. Bearings on cars are designed for a specific load. Manufacturers are not fond of building very much above minimal requirements. The result is that anything you do to increase those loads can rapidly approach the intolerable level. That means danger. If you must increase positive offset, keep it as small as possible, less than 1½ inches.

Some owners use spacers between the wheel and axle mounting surface as a way to obtain positive offset without buying new wheels. Spacers must only be used when proper wheels cannot be obtained, and then only for very small amounts of offset. Consider ½-inch spacers as the absolute maximum. Spacers are often poorly designed and constructed and can be dangerous. Even under the best of conditions, spacers impose unusual loads on wheels and lug nuts and can cause them to break. Never use spacers without also installing longer wheel studs and lug nuts of the strongest design possible.

Reject any spacer that does not make contact over the same area on the mounting surfaces as did the wheel alone. Inadequate contact surface can cause the wheel to flex and break. Wheel studs must be long enough so that lug nuts fully engage the threads. The studs must also have an unthreaded portion of the shank in contact with the spacer and wheel and fit snugly with the holes in the wheel. Failure to do so can impose bending loads on the stud bolts and cause them to fail.

It should not be necessary to mention that a stack of washers must never be used as a wheel spacer, but some owners have tried it. Repeat: *Never use a stack of washers as a wheel spacer*.

Another bad practice is using an adapter to change from one bolt pattern to another. Many of these adapters are poorly designed and poorly constructed. Too many of them fail under hard cornering, the worst possible time for failure. Spend the money for the proper wheels.

Street wheels and racing wheels are often similar in appearance but differ significantly in design and construction. Racing wheels are built to be as light as possible. This often means they have a small safety factor. Racers can accept this compromise as part of the cost of winning. You can't afford to take the risk. In your case, the cost of losing is too great.

Street wheels are designed for different conditions than racing wheels. The safety factor must be high enough to endure such conditions as overloading, severe bumps, contact with the curb, and corrosion from chemicals in the atmosphere. The result might be a wheel that is heavier than necessary but safe. For an assurance that the wheels you buy are safe, insist that they have the seal of approval of the Specialty Equipment Manufacturers Association (SEMA).

OEM wheels and some custom wheels are made of sheet steel. The rim is rolled to shape on a heavy mandrel. The center section is stamped to shape, and the two sections are then either welded or riveted together. The result is a light, low cost wheel that is adequate for average use. However, it might lack lateral stiffness and is usually not up to the stresses of road racing over a long period. If you want wider wheels and can be content with steel wheels, you might find what you want at your car dealer or a salvage shop. Carefully compare the offset, bolt pattern, bolt circle, and size of center hole to be sure the new wheels will fit properly.

Most custom wheels are made of cast aluminum. There are many companies making cast aluminum wheels. If they carry the SEMA stamp of approval, you can assume that any of them is adequately strong. Most differ only in appearance. To be honest, I should say that appearance is the main factor in most owners' choices of wheels. Figure 6-6 shows some wheel designs available at almost any performance shop.

Fig. 6-6. The variety of custom wheels is large. These are only a few that are available in any wheel or performance shop.

TIRE INFLATION

Proper tire inflation has several effects. One is directly related to load carrying capacity. Most tires are rated to carry their maximum load at an inflation pressure of 32 lbs. If your car has a front end weight of 1,800 lbs. and each tire has a maximum load capacity of 1,500 lbs. at 32 lbs. of pressure, you're in good condition. But if each tire is rated for 900 lbs. at that pressure, you are in trouble. You are operating at the maximum load for your tires. At that point tire wear will increase rapidly and safety will decrease. Although tires do not have to be inflated to their maximum rated pressures, they must be inflated sufficiently for the load they carry. A margin of safety is always desirable.

Inflation pressure also affects the shape of the tire. Correct inflation lets the tire tread contact the pavement evenly across its width. Overinflation causes the center of the tread to bulge out and raise the tread shoulders slightly. The result is rapid wear on the center of the tread. Underinflation has the opposite effect: the weight is carried mainly on the tread shoulders and the center tends to recede from the pavement surface. The result is rapid wear of the tread shoulders. Either condition reduces total tread wear and traction. Find out how much your car actually weighs on each axle. Determine the amount of inflation pressure your tires need for that weight and a reasonable margin of safety. Your tire dealer has a chart giving the information. Make a practice of checking tire pressures regularly. Once a week is best.

Tires that are underinflated cause handling problems. Steering begins to feel sloppy. What is happening is that the tire sidewalls lose their firmness as pressure decreases. The car has a tendency to float from side to side. On corners the tires roll under and cornering power decreases. If sufficiently underinflated, the tires can be pulled loose from the rim, losing air as if the tire had blown out.

Underinflation also increases the rolling resistance of the tire by permitting excessive flexing. This is more of a problem with bias-ply tires than with radials which are built with low rolling resistance. Both cases are undesirable, however. Underinflated bias-ply tires reduce tire life and increase fuel consumption. Underinflated radials destroy themselves slowly. The effect might not be apparent for several thousand miles, when they suddenly fail for no apparent reason. The reason was destruction from heat resulting from chronic underinflation.

Always check tire pressure when the tires are cool. Pressure will increase by as much as five pounds as the tire warms up under normal use. Never release air pressure from a warm or hot tire. Doing so results in additional heat and destruction of the tire.

TIRE ECONOMY

At present prices—mid-1988—a set of tires might cost as little as $125 or more than $400. Neither is an insignificant figure for most of us. Not long ago I read that the average tire life for American cars was 8,000 miles. Since I seldom get less than 45,000 miles on a tire and most drivers I know do about as well, there is a great discrepancy somewhere. What makes the difference? Some of it has to do with the quality of tires sold, but I usually do not buy the top-priced tires.

Stand near a busy intersection for an hour and watch the drivers. You will get an idea of some of the reasons why many tires wear out in less than 8,000 miles. The problem isn't speed; it's driving habits and tire care. Any driver can ruin a tire within 100 miles by driving it seriously underinflated. Look at the black streaks on the pavement near stoplights and favorite meeting spots and you will see other reasons. Listen to the painful sounds of squealing tires and you will find more.

Any time you manage to get a squeal of protest from your tires you can be sure you have just shortened the time before you will be visiting a tire store. That squeal can come from a sudden stop, a too fast corner, or trying to imitate a rocket takeoff. At the price of tires today, none of those maneuvers is terribly smart.

The question of cheap tires and safety comes up frequently. Are cheap tires inferior? Are they unsafe? Are expensive tires worth the additional money? The answers are yes, maybe, and sometimes.

Cheap tires are cheap because something was left out or substituted. A lower grade of ply fabric or rubber was used. The tire industry is one of the most fiercely competitive industries in the world. There is simply no way that a tire manufacturer can sell a top-quality tire at an economy price. That doesn't mean that a tire that sells for $100 is a better tire than one of another brand selling for $90. It does mean that either of those tires is better than one selling for $40. Higher priced tires cost more because of the quality of materials used in construction and because of the design of the tire. Radial tires cost more than bias-ply tires. Belted tires cost more than tires that are not belted.

Within the last few years tire manufacturers have been required by the U.S. Department of Transportation to test their tires for tread wear, traction, and ability to withstand the effects of high speed. The ratings are molded into the sidewalls of the tires. Traction grades are A, B, and C with A being the highest and C the lowest. Temperature ratings are also A, B, and C. The grades represent the tire's resistance to the generation of heat and its ability to dissipate heat when tested under controlled, laboratory conditions.

Grade C is the minimum rating required of all tires under the Federal Motor Safety Standard 109. Grades B and A represent higher levels of performance with A being the highest. Tread wear ratings are numerical with grade 150 representing a tread wear 1½ times that of grade 100. Additionally, some high performance tires carry a speed rating. Speed ratings were developed in Europe in response to the very high speeds permitted on some of their superhighways. Ask your dealer about the speed ratings of interest to you.

As might be expected, tires with high ratings generally cost more than lower rated tires. Should you insist on highly rated tires? Not necessarily. The use of the automobile should dictate the quality of tires installed. It makes little sense to buy the best tires available for a car that will be used only locally and never driven more than 40 mph. It makes just as little sense to buy a low rated tire for a car that will be driven longer distances at highway speeds in hot weather. Under these conditions the additional cost of a high rated tire is an inexpensive way to avoid injury or death.

FRONT-END ALIGNMENT

The three factors of main concern in front-end alignment are camber, toe, and caster. The correct adjustment of each is critical to good handling of a car.

On most cars and trucks the front, and sometimes the rear wheels, slant away from the vertical. As Fig. 6-7 shows, if the wheel slants out at the top, it is said to have positive camber. A wheel that slants in at the top has negative camber. Camber is stated as the number of degrees from vertical that the wheel slants. Years ago, cars had tires that were more nearly circular in cross-section than those in use today. Camber was designed into the front end to assist in balancing steering forces. Modern tires have treads that are wide and flat where they contact the pavement. Tilting the wheel causes the tread to lift on one side, reducing traction. Camber in modern cars is used more to keep the tire treads flat against the pavement as the wheel moves up and down than to assist in steering. Just as every load calls for optimum tire pressure, driving conditions, and tire design, every load also requires an optimum camber angle. Theoretically, changing tire design should require a change in camber angle. In practice, minor changes in tire design can be accommodated with no changes in camber angle. Generally, camber should be adjusted so that the outside wheel in a turn will have nearly zero camber.

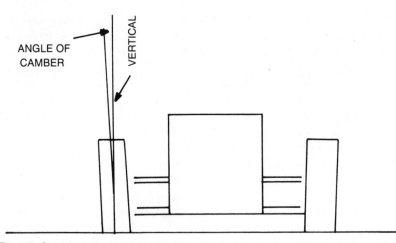

ANGLE OF
CAMBER

VERTICAL

Fig. 6-7. Camber is the angle that the tire and wheel centerline differs from the vertical. A wheel with positive camber tilts out at the top.

The ideal adjustment would give zero camber under all conditions of driving. Obviously, this is not possible because of the vertical movement of the wheel in response to bumps and the roll of the body during turns. Changes in adjustment should be small and carefully tested. Start with the manufacturer's setting if possible. If that setting is unknown, start with zero camber. Adjustments in camber are usually made by adding or removing shims or with an eccentric bushing. Check the manual for your car to determine how it's done on yours.

TOE-IN

Most owners unfamiliar with front end alignment would likely assume that the front wheels were exactly parallel when looked at from above. In practice, they aren't. The wheels are adjusted so that they are either closer together in the front or the rear of the wheels. The difference is called toe. If the front edges are closer together than the rear, the setting is called toe-in. Most cars are adjusted to have toe-in. Figure 6-8 shows a car with toe-in.

One reason for toe-in has to do with the forces of drag at work on the tires. Imagine a car with zero toe, the wheels exactly parallel, moving down the highway at speed. The front wheels resist being pushed. Rolling friction and other forces resist the forward motion of the car. There is always some flexing in the suspension system from the myriad bushings involved, each with its own tolerances. As a result the front of each tire tends to be pulled outward (in a toe-out position). Toe-out causes the tires to move in an angle to the forward motion of the car, and it scrubs rubber off the tire.

A more important problem is the steering effect of toe-out. Each wheel is turned away from the direction the car is taking. Each wheel is exerting a turning force. The problem is slight so long as the two turning forces are equal, but a bump or gust of wind or a slight movement of the steering wheel unbalances

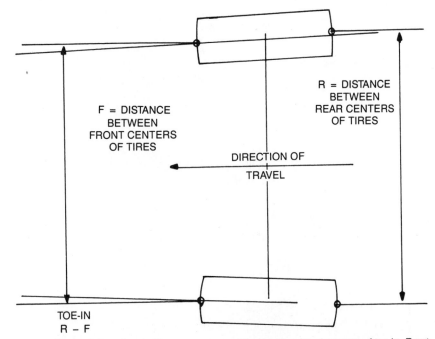

Fig. 6-8. Front wheels of rear drive cars are usually set with a small amount of toe-in. Front drive cars often have toe-out.

the turning forces. One tire then exerts more force than the other and tries to steer the car. The result is constant motion or wander of the car. Some initial toe-in is selected to counteract the built-in tolerances with the goal of achieving zero toe when the car is in motion. Additional toe-in is sometimes used to give a bit of initial understeer when the car is entering a corner.

Because the propelling forces on front wheel drive cars are greater than the drag forces, many front wheel drive cars are set with initial toe-out. The goal is to have the propelling forces pull the wheels into zero or slight toe-in under driving conditions.

Toe is usually adjusted by changing the length of the tie rods. Tie rods have left-hand threads on one end and right-hand threads on the other. By loosening the clamps and turning the rod, you can lengthen or shorten the rod. Check the manual for your car for the exact method. Also check for the suggested amount of toe. Start with the manufacturer's recommendations and make small adjustments.

CASTER ANGLE

If you could stand to one side of your car and view the points on which the front wheel pivots as it turns, you would see that a line through those points is not vertical to the ground. The angle between that line and the vertical line passing through the center of the wheel is the caster angle. Figure 6-9 shows caster angle. Caster is used to give a self-centering force to the steering. With

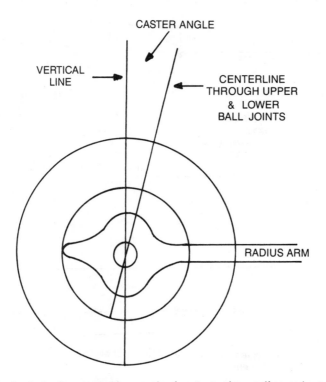

CASTER ANGLE

VERTICAL LINE

CENTERLINE THROUGH UPPER & LOWER BALL JOINTS

RADIUS ARM

Fig. 6-9. The front wheels are set with an angle of caster to give a self-centering action.

proper caster, the wheels return to center when the steering wheel is released. Too little caster causes the car to continue turning. Too much caster adds to the force needed to effect a turn. Adjusting caster requires a precision instrument that is a bit expensive. Getting an alignment shop to measure and adjust caster for you is probably better than trying to do it yourself.

All three adjustments to the alignment are important to proper handling and tire wear. Hitting bumps at high speed can distort various parts of the suspension system sufficiently to affect the adjustments. Wear of suspension parts also can change the adjustments. Make regular checks to be sure that suspension and steering parts are in correct adjustment. Can you do them yourself? Certainly, if you have the manuals, the equipment, and the skill. Adjustments of toe and camber are within the capability of most owners. Because of the precision tool required to measure caster, it is probably best to leave caster adjustment to an alignment shop. As a matter of fact, I feel so strongly about the requirement for accuracy in all alignment adjustments that I leave them all to a first-rate alignment shop. The small cost once a year is worth it.

7
CHAPTER

Brakes

ENGINES ARE MUCH MORE GLAMOROUS THAN BRAKES. ENGINES MAKE A LOT OF noise (so do some brakes!), and they make you go like the proverbial bat. It's easy to talk about displacements and compression ratios and blowers. Car owners get turned on by engine talk, but when was the last time you heard a driver brag about his brakes? "Boy, I touched that pedal, and those suckers brought me right down from 85 to whoa in five seconds. Never even wiggled. A straight line, just like an arrow." Sure. And yet, it's a very rare engine that has ever saved anyone's life. Brakes do it all the time. A basic law of vehicle performance is:

DON'T MAKE IT GO IF YOU CAN'T STOP IT

I like to drive fast. I long for the days when the speed limit on expressways was 70 and no one bothered you at 75. There are few feelings better than safely driving at high speed, feeling the power of a good engine, the smooth response of a well-tuned suspension system, all wheels balanced. Fantastic. But there is little that can take the edge off that feeling quicker than seeing a knot of traffic ahead, touching the brakes, and getting no response. Even with bad brakes there is some response, but it is so much less than what is needed that you get the feeling the car has actually accelerated. Downsville.

Good brakes are as important to high performance as a good engine. The stories of races lost by excellent cars that lost their brakes are legion. The number of lives lost because of brake failure will never be known, but it is tragically high. A good brake system might not make your car go faster, but it can certainly make going faster safer. As the man said, "Don't leave home without it."

HOW BRAKES WORK

A good brake system is a combination of many factors. Not one of them is sufficient by itself. Just as in an engine, all the factors must be working together harmoniously to make a good system. Since we have to start somewhere, let's start with the principles of operation.

Brakes are a mystery to most of us. Somehow we know that when things work right there is a connection between the pressure we put on the pedal and how fast the rig stops. We also know that sometimes there is a nasty noise that seems to come from the brakes. We might know that somewhere in the system there is some fluid that occasionally needs replenishing. And eventually we come to know about the expense of repair.

In order for us to get our cars to move down the road we have to use some form of energy. By pressing on the accelerator we ask the engine to burn some fuel and convert the energy in that burning fuel to forward motion of the rig. Some of that energy is stored in the forward motion. If we want to stop the vehicle fairly quickly we have to convert that stored energy to another form. In this case we convert it to heat by creating additional friction at the wheels. Creating that friction is the task of the brake system.

What happens is that when we press the brake pedal the pressure of our foot is transferred through fluid in steel lines to cylinders at each wheel. Those cylinders convert the pressure back into movement and force a high friction material (brake shoes and pads) into contact with a moving element (brake drums and rotors). The drums or rotors are fastened to the back of the wheels

Fig. 7-1. By using a special gauge, a mechanic can determine whether a brake drum is warped out of round.

and turn with the wheels. The friction we have just induced forces the wheels to slow down and bring the vehicle to a stop.

One product of all that friction is heat, lots of it. Another product of the friction is wear on all the contacting parts. That's why brakes wear out. Eventually the friction material on the brake shoes and pads wears to the point that they are no longer effective. The cast iron drums and rotors also wear. Sometimes they warp as a result of the very high temperatures resulting from all that heat. Usually the drums and rotors can be restored to serviceable condition by ''turning'' them in a lathe. A very small amount of the surface metal is removed to bring the surface back to original condition. Figure 7-1 shows a mechanic using a special gauge to check a brake drum for warping.

CHOOSING BRAKE FRICTION MATERIALS

Every one of us eventually has to face the fact that the brakes on our cars and trucks need service. Or we might be working on the brakes for the same reason we're doing other work on the car, to improve performance and handling. What kind of linings or pads should you ask for? I talked with some brake experts and contacted some brake manufacturers. Here's what I found.

The choices used to be organic (asbestos), semimetallic, and sintered metal. Well, you didn't think it would be easy, did you? Everybody has his own language. Hang in there—it isn't so bad.

Traditionally, asbestos has been the material of choice for brake friction materials. It has several things going for it. It is resistant to heat. It develops lots of friction, and it is cheap, very cheap. We have recently found out that it is also very dangerous.

But even before we found out it was dangerous, we had discovered that asbestos was less than satisfactory in some brake installations. When asbestos gets hot it tends to lose some of its friction. This can happen at high vehicle speeds or with repeated braking when you're coming down mountains or carrying heavy loads. Many different attempts have been made to counteract these problems by using fillers such as limestone and clay and various metal powders.

Another approach is to take various kinds of metallic powders and use very high temperatures to melt them together to form a product called sintered metal. Sintered metal brakes have superior resistance to heat and long wear. But—those compromises again—they tend to be noisy, wear the brake drums rapidly, and exercise very low stopping power until warmed up. Most experienced drivers with sintered metal brakes ride the pedal for a few minutes when they first start up to warm the brakes.

Another material which has become very popular is made by pressing various fibers and metallic powders with bonding agents in molds under very high pressure. The result is semimetallic brake material. Since semimetallic has friction characteristics superior to asbestos and does not degrade the brake drums and rotors as rapidly as sintered metal, it is becoming widely used.

With all these choices, guess what I was told when I asked for a recommendation on materials. The manufacturers and the brake specialists all said, ''Use the same materials originally used on your vehicle.'' I find that a less than satis-factory answer because I know that manufacturers like to use the least expensive product that will just give acceptable performance. From what I've been able to learn about the various products, I recommend semimetallic if it can be had for your brakes. If not, ask for the best possible quality organic materials.

As mentioned earlier in chapter 1, the government recently eliminated asbestos from the choices. It ruled that asbestos is too dangerous to have around. Asbestos forms dust easily when handled or machined. When inhaled, the dust has been found to encourage the development of lung cancer. So no more asbestos brake materials are available. In this case the government did something we can all agree with.

WHICH BRAKE FLUID

Originally, vehicle brakes consisted of something like a boat anchor, a heavy weight attached to the vehicle by a rope or chain. When you wanted to stop, you threw out the anchor. Next came a brake shoe operated by a long lever. You simply reached over and pulled on the lever, which moved the brake shoe against the outer surface of the wheel. At slow speeds the system was effective. As the horse was displaced by an engine and speeds increased, brakes had to be improved. A brake drum was attached to the axle with friction material resembling a belt encircling the drum. Applying the brakes by either a lever or a foot pedal tightened the belt around the drum. A linkage of cables or rods transmitted the force from the lever or pedal to the belt.

A problem with the above mechanical systems was that sometimes the brakes needed to be applied while the car was going around a corner. Engineers had a difficult time designing a system of rods and levers that would smoothly transmit the braking force under all conditions of wheel turning and bouncing. Cable-actuated brakes were better than rod-actuated systems, but they left something to be desired. One problem with cable brakes was that rust had a habit of forming between the cable and its shield, causing the brakes to bind.

In the mid-1920s engineers developed hydraulic brakes. Tubes and flexible hoses filled with fluid were used to transmit the pedal or lever force to the brakes. Since the hoses could flex with wheel movement, it made no difference what position the wheel was in; braking action was always smooth. As might be expected, many engineers and car manufacturers resisted the newfangled hydraulic brakes. Advertising materials of the day often referred to them as dangerous, suggesting that the tubing and hoses would easily rupture, causing a loss of brakes. However, all manufacturers eventually came to recognize the superiority of hydraulic brakes. Ford was among the last, using cable brakes until just before World War II.

Hydraulic brakes, of course, require the use of some sort of fluid to transmit the pressure from the brake pedal to the wheels. It has to be a special fluid that retains its consistency without regard for extreme temperature changes. It must be compatible with the rubber seals used in brake cylinders. And it should not be corrosive.

Meeting all these demands is not as easy as it might seem. The glycol-based brake fluid commonly used meets the requirements, but it does have one problem. Glycol has an affinity for water. It's true that the system is sealed, but there is always some slight air movement in and out of the system at the fluid reservoir. You take the cover off to check the fluid level, and air enters. Air contains moisture, which is absorbed by the fluid. Also that can of fluid you keep in your shop to fill the reservoir gets air and moisture in when you open it. The moisture finds its way into the brake system and causes problems.

You might have heard of a new kind of brake fluid that doesn't absorb moisture, silicone-based brake fluid. Since it doesn't absorb moisture, using silicone fluid should eliminate the rusting in rear brake cylinders. It also boils at a higher temperature than the glycol-based fluid commonly used. Shouldn't we use it? Not necessarily. Like many things that appear to be magic answers, this one has some disadvantages. One is that silicone-based fluid compresses up to four times as much as glycol-based fluid. That tends to give a mushy feel to the brakes, as if they had air in the lines. Another is that this effect is increased at higher altitudes, not a good thing to have. It appears that for now the older, glycol-based fluid is better.

There are two of these fluids that can be used: DOT 3 and DOT 4. The DOT refers to the Department of Transportation, which sets the standards for most things automotive. Unless it has absorbed water, DOT 3 fluid boils at 401 degrees and DOT 4 boils at 446 degrees. There will always be some moisture present, causing the boiling points to be reduced to 284 degrees and 311 degrees, respectively. DOT 3 and DOT 4 can be mixed. But never mix either with DOT 5, the silicone-based material. Also, never-*NEVER-NEVER* add any kind of petroleum product to your brake fluid. The rubber seals would quickly disintegrate and your brakes would fail.

From looking at the various components of your brake system you might not guess that it is really a sensitive system. Don't add any contaminant to the system. We've already mentioned the problem with moisture, but there are other contaminants. The master cylinder and fluid reservoir are the most frequently serviced components in the brake system. They are also located in a dirty environment, the engine room. Unless you bathe your engine every day, an unlikely routine, the whole area under the hood is dirty. Oil vapors escape and settle on every surface. Road dust and grime settle on the oil. Messy. Opening the brake fluid reservoir is an invitation to some of that grime to enter and make itself at home. Believe me, road grime or any kind of material other than the correct brake fluid is not a pleasant guest in the brake system. Before removing the reservoir cover, take a moment to wipe the cover and surrounding surfaces with a rag.

HOW TO KNOW IF YOUR BRAKES ARE BAD

There are two approaches to knowing when to service your brakes. The most common one is to wait until they announce their impending demise by growling loudly. The growling is the sound made when metal grinds against metal. At that point you can be assured that your brakes need service. See Fig. 7-2. You can also be assured that the required service is going to be expensive. By the time the growling starts, the friction material has been worn away and the contacting surfaces are eating themselves up. Part of those surfaces is going to be replaced anyway, so what's the problem? The problem is that the parts that would normally be retained are expensive to replace. Excessive wear caused by metal-to-metal contact assures that replacement will be necessary. Normal wear usually requires only inexpensive resurfacing.

The second method of determining when your brakes need service is routine inspection. Inspection of the pads on disc brakes is usually easy. On many cars, if you look closely, you can see the edge of the pads from the front of the car. If the pad shows at least ⅛ inch of friction material remaining, your brakes are all right. Inspecting drum brakes requires removal of the wheel and brake drum. That's an easy job on most recent models. If you're not sure how it's done on your car, check your manual. If the friction material is riveted on the brake shoes, the friction material should never be permitted to wear down to the rivet heads. If the material is glued to the shoes, make an appointment for service when the friction material shows less than ⅛ inch remaining at the thinnest point.

How often should you inspect your brakes? Because the rate of wear depends so heavily on your driving habits, there is no easy answer. Unless you know from previous experience that your brakes normally last much longer, I

Fig. 7-2. If brake pads are permitted to wear down to the point that metal-to-metal contact occurs, the rotor or drum will be damaged.

suggest you inspect them for the first time at 20,000 miles. If little wear is present, inspect again at 40,000 miles. When wear gets close to the replacement point, an inspection every 5,000 miles is prudent.

There are other indications that all is not well with your brakes. If there is any kind of malfunction such as a pulsating pedal, grinding noises, pulling to one side, or grabbing, get an inspection immediately. The problem might be simple and the repair inexpensive. Pulling or grabbing brakes can cause you to have an accident. Grinding noises indicate that something in the system is making metal-to-metal contact and eating itself up. Figure 7-3 shows what happens when disc brakes drag for a long period of time. A pulsating pedal usually means a rotor or brake drum has warped, causing the pressure to vary as the wheel turns. In all these cases, correction is needed. A rule of thumb in any mechanical malfunction is: *The longer the malfunction is allowed to exist, the more expensive it will be to repair.* Get it fixed now.

Someone is bound to ask, "What about those built-in systems that are supposed to make some sort of noise to let you know the friction materials are ready for service?" Well, I've driven nearly a million miles and I'm still listening. So far, I haven't heard any signals from my brakes.

Another question is, "Do you have to replace the shoes or pads on all four wheels every time?" Not unless they need it. Most honest mechanics will tell you that a set of rear brakes will probably last as long as two sets of front brakes. I have found that this is usually true.

Fig. 7-3. These brakes had been dragging for many miles because their calipers rusted so badly they did not release. The result is two ruined rotors and a large repair bill.

If you don't want to inspect your brakes yourself, any mechanic can do it for you for a small labor charge. I'm aware that there are a lot of brake and muffler shops that advertise free brake inspections. I'm skeptical of them. As a result of their free inspections I've had them tell me that my shocks were worn out when they were nearly new, that my brakes were dangerously worn when there was nothing wrong with them, and that suspension parts needed to be replaced long before they were worn out. Friends have told me similar stories. Most owners haven't the haziest notion of the condition of their cars. They are easy to convince that wear exists when it doesn't. Not all the shops who advertise free inspections are dishonest, but I don't know how to tell the difference. Take your car to a mechanic you have dealt with and can trust. If you have questions about the condition of your car's systems, he will be glad to show you why he makes his recommendations.

FINDING A MECHANIC YOU CAN TRUST

Finding a mechanic you can trust is often like finding a doctor or hairdresser. There are lots of them out there and most are good. Finding the one you want to work with can be a problem. I found a way that works for me. When I move to a new area I go to a few large parts stores and ask for the name of the best mechanic in town. Ask around and you will begin to hear the same names. Then check those names out. Nose around their shops without getting in the way. A good mechanic will have a clean, organized shop. He will be busy. He will have ample room to work. His tools will show that they are cared for. Parts will not be strewn all over.

Describe what you want done or what's wrong with your car and listen. A good mechanic will be able to give you a clear description of the probable cause of the problem and how it can be repaired and about how much it will cost. He will also give you a close estimate of when it will be finished. When you find one of these paragons, nurture the relationship. Ask thoughtful questions, but don't hang on his arm. His time is valuable. When he does a good job, don't complain about the cost. And, above all, tell him how much you appreciate the quality of work he does.

INSPECT THE BRAKE LINES

Frequent inspection of the brake lines is also a good idea. The flexible portions of the lines are especially subject to wear. Be sure that no part of the lines rubs against any surface. Look for signs of leaking fluid all along the lines and at the wheel cylinders. In older vehicles, watch for signs of rust on the steel lines. Rust is especially likely to occur under the clamps holding the steel lines to the frame. Leaking at any point in the system requires immediate repair. A rusty brake line is a tragedy waiting for the worst possible time.

Brake lines must always be replaced with top quality materials. Never use copper tubing. Preflared steel tubing of different lengths is available at parts shops. Use it. Never try to make your own flares. The commonly available flaring tools are not capable of making the special flares needed for safety. Consider replacing the rubber hoses with steel-braided flex hoses. These hoses resist the expansion pressure of the fluid better than rubber. The result is firmer brakes.

Fluid often escapes from the system over a period of time. If the fluid level in the reservoir gets too low, air enters the system. Air is very compressible and makes for soft, spongy brakes. Regular refilling of the reservoir avoids the problem. If air does get into your brake system, it must be removed by bleeding. Bleeding brakes requires either two persons or an expensive pressure tool. A friend is cheaper. Start by filling the reservoir. At each wheel cylinder there is a nipple that can be loosened to permit fluid and air to escape. Bleeding brakes is a simple operation, but it must be done correctly, or the situation will be made worse rather than better.

Find a buddy with a heavy foot who can follow simple instructions. Tell him to push the brake pedal slowly all the way to the floor and hold it when you say "Push." When the pedal reaches the floor, he is to say "Down" and hold the pedal until you say "Up." Now you crawl under the car with a small wrench (you'll have to discover the size), and locate the bleeder valve on the wheel cylinder. Tell him to push. You open the bleeder valve enough to permit fluid to escape. When he says "Down," you close the valve and say "Up." When he releases the pedal you start the operation over. Repeat five or six times or until there are no more air bubbles. Then move to the next wheel. All four wheel cylinders will have to be bled to get all the air out. After bleeding a couple of wheels, it is a good idea to refill the reservoir. When you have bled all four wheels, top off the reservoir.

WHAT MAKES A GOOD BRAKE JOB

A good brake job should return your brakes to nearly the same condition as when the car left the factory. The only difference will be that some parts will be reconditioned rather than new. If you have followed the suggestions above for inspecting your brakes, your rotors and drums can very likely be used again. Usually, turning them on a special lathe will correct a warp caused by extreme heat. Even if there is no warping, there will be tiny grooves worn in the metal surface. See Fig. 7-4. Some owners believe that it is not necessary to remove these grooves if they are not deep.

I asked some experts whether it is essential to turn the drums and rotors if surface wear is not extreme. There were differing answers. One expert with 31 years' experience on brake systems said that the high polish resulting from the wear needs to be removed to avoid squeal. Another said that if wear is not extreme the only reason to turn drums and rotors is to eliminate an existing squeal or a pulsating pedal caused by warped drums or rotors. My feeling from talking with them is that the small additional cost of reconditioning the drums and rotors is well worth it since removing the polish also increases the friction effectiveness of the metal parts. Figure 7-5 shows a drum that a mechanic has reconditioned by turning on a special lathe.

Fig. 7-4. This partially turned rotor shows the difference between the worn surface and the reconditioned surface.

Other parts that might need servicing are the wheel cylinders and calipers. The wheel cylinders and pistons inside those cylinders transfer the pedal pressure into movement of the brake shoes in the rear wheels. Since the cylinders are continually filled with brake fluid—a fairly good lubricant—and effectively sealed from the outside, it would seem that there should be minimal wear, not enough to bother with. Actually, there is very little wear to the metal parts but there is a need for servicing the cylinders. Always? My expert said yes in 90 percent of the cases. Here's why.

Earlier I mentioned that brake fluid has an affinity with water. Air enters the system any time the cover is removed from the reservoir. Some water is absorbed by the fluid in the container standing on the shelf in your garage. You add a bit of moisture every time you add fluid. The condensed water is heavier than the brake fluid and works its way down to the lowest point in the brake system, the bottom of the wheel cylinders. Once there, it causes the formation of rust in the cylinders. The rust surface is rough. When you apply the brakes the rubber seals that fit into the cylinders move across that rough surface and are worn. Eventually they leak. Some of the leaking fluid gets on the brake shoes and drums. Trouble. Get those cylinders serviced every time you put in new brake shoes.

The situation with the disc brakes on your front wheels is different. The rust develops here, too, but in this case the rubber seals don't move and develop leaks. So that isn't usually a problem. Moreover, the disc brake pistons

Fig. 7-5. The mechanic reconditioned this drum by turning on a special lathe. The resulting surface gives good braking action.

don't have the same amount of travel as the rear brake pistons. They are not continually moving over that rough surface. But the calipers, those parts which apply the pressure to the rotors, can get very rusty. This is especially true if you live in the northern part of the country where huge amounts of salt are applied to your car every winter. That rust might build up to the point that the calipers can't move freely. The result is either a dragging brake or diminished braking to one wheel. It doesn't always happen. My experts both said that 90 percent of the time front disc brake actuating systems would not need servicing. Leave the decision to your mechanic.

CAN YOU REPAIR YOUR BRAKES?

Doing a brake job is traditionally one of the repairs that owners perform themselves. With the exception of the lathes needed for turning rotors and drums, there is no expensive equipment required. Reamers for servicing wheel cylinders are not expensive and are not difficult to use. There are one or two small hand tools that will be needed, but they are not expensive. Check your manual for these. You will need at least two good, sturdy stands to hold the end of the car you're working on. Remember, never use jacks to support a car while any part of your body is under it. And you'll need the normal wrenches and pliers you would use for any repair job.

I would suggest that you always have the rotors and drums turned. The cost is minimal and the results are well worth it. Take them to one of the machine shops in your area that specialize in automotive work. Your mechanic would probably do them for you, too. Most independent mechanics have no objection to doing that sort of work for their regular customers.

Okay, assume now that you've got your brakes installed. There is one more thing that needs to be considered. Brakes must be properly broken in. Too many drivers take a new brake job and run up to 70 and stomp on the brakes to see if the mechanic did it right. He could have used the best materials and precision labor, and those brakes are headed down the drain. For the first 200 miles, brakes should be used lightly. They are never shaped to fit the brake drums and rotors precisely. Light application for a couple of hundred miles permits the high spots to wear down and shape to fit. Heavy pressure and the resulting high heat on high spots of brand new brakes glaze the materials. Figure 7-6 shows a brake shoe that was glazed as a result of heavy braking. The result is less than satisfactory brakes and noise. Break them in.

One of the driver's worst frights is to have his brakes fail. That's the stuff of nightmares. Having an understanding of how your brakes work and how to keep them working can help to change the nightmare into a pleasant dream. No program for improving the performance and handling of a car or truck is complete without doing the brakes.

Fig. 7-6. Glazed brake shoe resulting from overheating of the brakes. Glazed surfaces develop less friction and braking power.

8
CHAPTER

Ignition—the Heart of Your Engine

THE BEST ENGINE IN THE WORLD—WITH FANCY MANIFOLDS AND INJECTORS, A whizbang turbocharger, the latest headers, and a super cam—is only an expensive boat anchor without a good ignition system. Dr. Christopher Jacobs, designer of ignition systems for some of the most sophisticated racing engines in the United States, has written that inadequate ignition or loss of ignition has been the cause of more lost races than any other factor. Without an ignition system, your engine won't run.

WHAT THE IGNITION SYSTEM DOES

Basically, your ignition system does two important things: it furnishes the energy literally to light the fire in the cylinders, and it furnishes that energy at the precisely correct time. Simple, huh? Well, consider that in an eight-cylinder engine running at 3,500 rpm, the ignition must light the fire 14,000 times per minute. The heat and pressure inside that cylinder where the fire is lit are tremendous. The fire must be lit with a precision of one degree each of those 14,000 times. Still sound simple? Okay, speed the engine up to 8,000 rpm for racing, and the match must be applied at precisely the right time under even worse conditions of heat and pressure 32,000 times per minute.

Then consider that most of us expect the ignition system to function flawlessly for thousands of miles with no maintenance or even a pat on the back. The manufacturer of one new engine suggests taking a look at the spark plugs every 50,000 miles. Some things get no respect. Let's take the time to give a little attention and respect to the heart of our engines.

MAIN PARTS OF THE IGNITION SYSTEM

Not all engines will have all the parts discussed here. Some of the newer models combine functions of one or more parts. But because many of our cars are older models, we'll start with some older systems.

The battery is seldom thought of as a part of the ignition system. Disconnect it, however, and the engine won't run. It's true that several years ago, when alternators first became popular, one manufacturer started a car, removed the battery, and had the car driven coast to coast without the battery. All tricks aside, there has to be some source of electrical energy for the ignition system. The battery is the easiest to use. (I'll mention magnetos later.)

Like the rest of the ignition system, the battery is often forgotten and neglected until it cries out for help. Look under the hood of most cars, and you will see the poor battery sitting down in the corner somewhere with grit and grime all over it. Its terminals are likely to be covered with a green growth that looks like something from a horror movie. Until the battery dies, or faints, we just ignore it.

We won't take the time to go into all the processes by which the battery works. It's sufficient here to say that the chemical reaction between the acid solution and the battery plates releases electricity. The chemical reaction changes the structure of the plates, and after a short time the reaction quits. No more energy is released. The alternator—or generator—reverses the reaction and restores the plates to their original condition. Well, not quite original condition. With every cycle, there is some loss of condition and eventually the battery can no longer be restored to a condition where it can function. We say the battery won't take a charge. The length of time before the battery reaches the failed condition varies. Failure can happen in a few hours, or it might take several years. The length of time depends on how the battery is cared for. Respect.

One rather mundane material in the battery is water. The water forms part of the acid solution and is essential to the operation of the type of battery used in cars. With every cycle of the battery, heat is produced. Some of the water tries to evaporate and, in most batteries, succeeds. If the water level is permitted to become too low, the battery can no longer function, nor can it be restored. Regular replacement of the water is essential. The best water to use is distilled water or mineral-free water. Minerals can contaminate the acid solution and impair the chemical process. Tap water can be used in an emergency.

So-called maintenance-free batteries have a water-entrapment process built in. The water evaporates, is trapped within the battery, and returns to the battery cells. Replacement of water is neither necessary nor possible with these batteries.

IGNITION COILS

Owners of hopped-up cars like to talk about their coils. They like to brag about the hot coils they're using. Look in any car magazine and you will see ads for coils with amazing amounts of voltage output. The numbers are impressive and sell a lot of coils. Because the only purpose of an ignition coil is to increase the voltage from battery level of 12 volts to several thousand volts, it is easy to fall for the notion that more is better. One result is the popularity of coils with an output of 40,000 volts or more. Is all that voltage necessary? Not really. Lost in all the advertising is the fact that voltage doesn't ignite the fuel mixture. Current or amperage is the energy that lights the fire. The spark could be 100,000 volts, but the fuel will not burn unless sufficient amperage is present.

Most owners don't know that only about 12,000 to 24,000 volts is necessary to get a spark across the electrodes in a spark plug. That's all. Increasing the voltage in a transformer or coil decreases the amperage. Those 40,000 volt coils cannot have the amperage of a 20,000 volt coil. That is a basic law of electricity. Then why are 40,000 volt coils so popular? Advertising. Selling 40,000 volts is easier than selling 20,000 volts. It's that simple.

But, if 12,000 volts are all that's necessary to light the fire, why have a 24,000 volt coil? Two reasons. One, spark voltage goes down as engine speed goes up. Additional voltage must be supplied to keep the engine running at high speed. The second reason is that engaging the starter reduces available voltage for firing the spark plugs. Because 24,000 volts is sufficient to light the fire at any engine speeds you can reach, there is no need to buy more. Remember, amperage goes down as voltage goes up, and amperage is what ignites the fuel mixture. When shopping for a coil, ask for amperage figures.

As the coil does its job of changing 12 volts to 24,000 volts, it generates heat. The windings in most coils are immersed in oil or some other fluid to help dissipate the heat. Some coils use a plastic case. Leave them on the shelf. Metal cases dissipate the heat faster and offer greater security against case damage.

A rippled surface on the coil terminal is an advantage. Electricity is always trying to escape to ground. Using a rippled surface on the terminal increases the distance to ground and holds the high tension or secondary wire more securely.

Spark energy requirements change as engine speed changes. One way to meet these changes is to use a coil with a variable permeability core. Sometimes these coils are advertised as being automatically controlled. A variable permeable core causes the coil output to change as the engine requirements change. I consider this feature of a coil to be very important.

Seldom can all these features be found in one coil. The Jacobs Compu*Coil is one that has them all. There might be others that I don't know about.

Older ignition systems with breaker points also use a condenser. When the breaker points open to fire the plugs, the primary current jumps across the open points. If this electrical charge were not directed elsewhere, the metal contacts of the points would become very hot and burn. The gap between the points would change rapidly and the points could no longer perform their job. The purpose of the condenser is to furnish a diversion for the electrical current when the points are open and prevent them from burning. Replacing the condenser when points are replaced is the best maintenance.

IGNITION DISTRIBUTORS

One-cylinder engines don't need a distributor. The spark energy can flow directly from the coil to the only spark plug. (I realize that one-cylinder engines use a totally different ignition system. Humor me for the sake of this illustration.) But very few of you will be driving a one-cylinder car. Directing the spark energy to the correct cylinder at the correct time is the function of the distributor. Inside the distributor is a rotor which is driven by the engine camshaft. As it turns, the rotor "points" toward terminals on the underside of the distributor cap as illustrated in Fig. 8-1. Each of those terminals, and its associated wire, feeds spark energy to a spark plug. The energy, released at the appropriate time by the breaker points or reluctor (see Fig. 8-2), flows from the coil to the center terminal of the distributor. From there it flows through the rotor to one of the terminals near the outer edge of the distributor cap and then to a spark plug. As mentioned earlier, all of this happens very rapidly with current flowing to a spark plug thousands of times per minute. Some owners, believing in the magic of money, are fond of buying expensive custom distributors for their engines. There is no debating the fact that chromed distributors look nice and fancy distributors are bragging material. Unfortunately for the fancy distributor set, most OEM distributors work just as well.

Earlier Fords with breaker points can usually install a Dura-Spark unit used from 1976 to 1982. Most early GM engines can use either the HEI #1103285 or #1111267. Chrysler engines 360 cubic inches and smaller can use Chrysler #3690428. The 440 engine uses #3690426. These are conversion kits to change to electronic ignition. Both of the Chrysler kits can be improved by using Autotronics distributor cap #8430 if there is enough room. This cap is larger than the OEM cap and decreases the chances of spark crossover inside the cap.

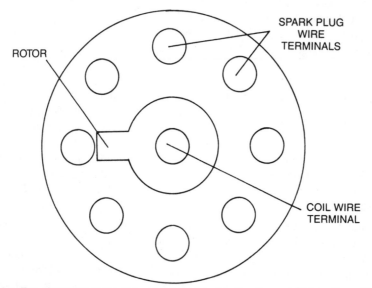

Fig. 8-1. The distributor rotor turns with the engine directing the current from the coil to the appropriate spark plug wire.

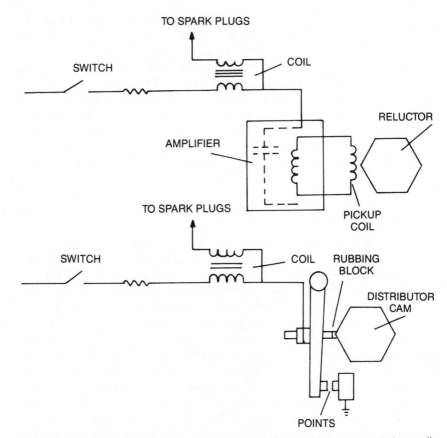

Fig. 8-2. The system at the top uses a reluctor to send a magnetic signal through the amplifier to "fire" the coil. This system is used in most cars since the 70s. The older breaker point system is shown at the bottom.

COMPUTER IGNITION SYSTEMS

The last few years have seen another ignition system, the computer system. As engines have become more sophisticated, their ignition requirements have increased. Engineers recognized that there was much more required than just a spark at the right time. Conditions within the cylinder at ignition are constantly changing, and the ignition requirements are, likewise, changing.

A fundamental law of ignition is that for any given combustion chamber condition there is an ideal spark. Too much or too little current is detrimental to the combustion process. As combustion proceeds, the electrical resistance across the spark gap changes. By measuring this resistance, an engineer can determine whether the spark current should be decreased or increased. Obviously, no engineer can make those thousands of measurements and corrections needed in the amount of time available. Nor could you have an engineer riding with you just for that purpose. A computer ignition system can handle the task of measuring the resistance changes and making the corrections. One ignition computer is programmed to make up to 33 measurements and adjustments for each cylinder firing in just 1½ degrees of rotation. Precise and correct ignition is virtually assured for all running conditions.

Most new cars are equipped with computer ignition systems. The ignition performance of older models can be brought up to a level equal to the best new engines if you add an aftermarket ignition computer. Installation is a simple matter of hooking up a few wires and attaching the computer to a convenient location. Jacobs Electronics and MSD are two manufacturers I know of who make excellent computer ignition systems. Both claim that even the performance of factory computer systems can be enhanced by the addition of their computers. I have no reason to believe otherwise.

SPARK PLUG WIRES

Spark plug wires have the important task of conducting the electrical current from the distributor to the spark plugs. In early cars, the wires were often bare strips of copper or brass. As engines became more sophisticated and ignition requirements became more stringent, insulation was added and different core materials were utilized. Some ''wires'' had no wire in them at all; their conducting material was a string of graphite or other conducting material.

One of the first additions required by any modified engine is high performance spark plug wires. There are strange things that happen to current flowing through spark plug wires. The greater the degree of engine modification, the more difficult it is to get the electrical energy to the spark plugs. The best wires have a fine wire wound in a spiral pattern around a ferrite or impregnated core. These wires eliminate the harmonic vibrations which plague stranded core wires. They also are much more durable and deliver more energy than fiber core wires.

The insulation on ignition wires is very important. Ignition wires work in a very hostile environment, the engine compartment. Vibrational level is high. Temperatures can run to hundreds of degrees. Rubber insulation is definitely not sufficient. Silicone insulation is probably the best buy for the money. Look for wires with spark plug boots vulcanized to the insulation.

SPARK PLUGS

The final element in the ignition process is the spark plug. Spark plugs come in different styles for different tasks. You have little choice over the size; your plugs must fit the holes in the cylinder heads. Nor can you choose whether to use gasket or gasketless plugs. The engineers decided that for you. Stick with their decision. The choices that are left are brand of plug, heat range, and extended or flush nose.

Let's take them in reverse order. The nose of a spark plug is right out there on the firing line, in the center of the combustion chamber. See Fig. 8-3. Having the firing point of the spark plug in the right location is important. The incoming charge is directed by the design of the intake manifold and valve pockets to

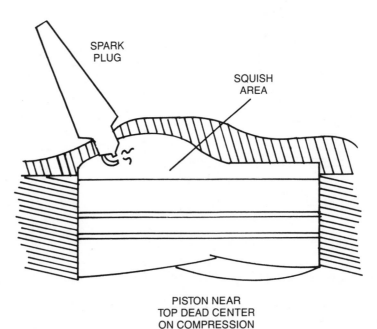

SPARK
PLUG

SQUISH
AREA

PISTON NEAR
TOP DEAD CENTER
ON COMPRESSION
STROKE

Fig. 8-3. The nose of the spark plug is located at the optimum point for best ignition of the fuel/air mixture.

move in a desired pattern in relation to the cylinder head shape and the piston head.

The engineers expect the combustion process to begin at an ideal location. They select the spark plug type which they believe will best perform that function. While it's best to stay with a spark plug with an extended nose if that's what the engineers designed for, you can experiment with plugs with flush or recessed noses if you wish. Figure 8-4 shows the different types of spark plug noses. However, because of the possibility of plug interference with the tops of the pistons, never use an extended nose plug in an engine not designed for it.

The length of the plug nose and the material used for the center electrode are the main materials affecting the heat range of the spark plug. The notion of hot and cold plugs is somewhat confusing. Figure 8-5 illustrates the difference between hot and cold plugs. Some owners think of hot and cold in terms of performance. With plugs it's a bit different. A hot plug is one with a design that tends to retain combustion heat. A cold plug is designed to dissipate that heat. The ideal temperature for a spark plug nose is about 700 degrees. If it gets much hotter than this it begins to glow and cause detonation. Detonation is the premature ignition of the fuel mixture. When an engine detonates, the mixture begins to burn before the piston reaches the ignition point. Severe detonation can ruin an engine in seconds.

If the plug runs much less than 700 degrees, carbon tends to build up. Ignition becomes erratic and the plugs require frequent cleaning. Stay with stock heat range plugs unless you have some good reason to try a colder plug. One

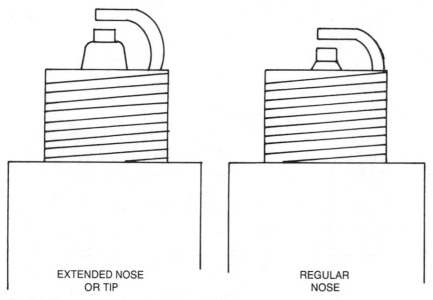

EXTENDED NOSE
OR TIP

REGULAR
NOSE

Fig. 8-4. The two types of spark plugs used most frequently are shown here. Notice the different lengths of noses.

reason would be adding a blower or raising the compression ratio. Another would be if the car is used almost entirely for fast, highway driving or for pulling a heavy trailer. If you believe you need a plug of a different heat range, try moving only one step at a time.

All brands of spark plugs were not created equal. Because of differences in electrode and nose materials there are differences in the plugs' susceptibility to fouling. There are also differences in the durability of the various brands. I happen to like Autolite plugs because they last longer than others in my engines. If my engines were worn to the point that they were burning oil, I would probably find Champions a bit better at handling the fouling.

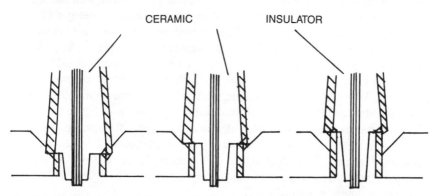

CERAMIC   INSULATOR

Fig. 8-5. Heat travels through the ceramic insulator to the metal body of the spark plug. The length of the heat path determines the heat range of the spark plug.

AFTERMARKET IGNITION SYSTEMS

There are only four things to discuss here; magnetos, performance distributors, computer ignition systems, and ping control systems. Let's take them in order.

Magnetos are a solution looking for a problem. In cars and trucks they have not found the problem. Magnetos have only one real application, engines without a battery system. They work fine for small engines on lawn mowers and boats and other applications that don't also have a battery. They would also work on a car that for some reason could not have a battery. Airplane engines use magnetos as a result of governmental fiat, not for engineering advantage. The FAA requires an ignition system separate from the general electrical system. That is a bureaucratically derived requirement that has lost its purpose in the dim past. The spark output of magnetos is inferior to battery ignition in nearly every way. Other than the above-mentioned situation in which no battery is permitted, there is really only one thing a magneto does well; it is very good at relieving unwary car owners of their hard-earned money.

There used to be a place for performance distributors in street vehicles. Some of the old point-condenser distributors were pretty bad. The new, electronic systems have overcome those deficiencies. With the possible exception of very high speed engines or older cars with a point-condenser ignition system, there just isn't much need for performance distributors anymore. If you have one of the older systems, you can improve its performance by substituting the correct electronic system as mentioned above. If you wish to retain the point-condenser system because of serviceability requirements due to your unique use, you might want to consider a dual point-distributor. Figure 8-6 shows a dual-point system. Other than that, thumbs down.

Computer ignition systems are a different ball game. Because of the factors discussed in the section on distributors, computers are generally desirable. They offer ignition superior to any other system in current use. Until you have used a good computer ignition system, you don't really know how much power your engine can have or how smoothly it can run. But any system can fail. If you buy a computer system, be sure to get one that permits return to the conventional system in the easiest possible manner. Figure 8-7 is an example of an aftermarket computer ignition system.

Ping control systems also offer real advantages for some special applications. I drive a van with a large engine that has been slightly modified. The major portion of driving is normal business and pleasure with a light load. Under those conditions I can run quite a bit more spark advance than normal. That gives me some improvement in mileage and power. On frequent weekends I use the van to pull a travel trailer weighing about 5,000 lbs. The engine runs hotter, and I cannot run so much spark advance. After trying several solutions, I installed a ping control system. Now I have the large advance for normal driving, and by simply turning a knob, I can get up to 15 degrees retard from that position. I like the flexibility.

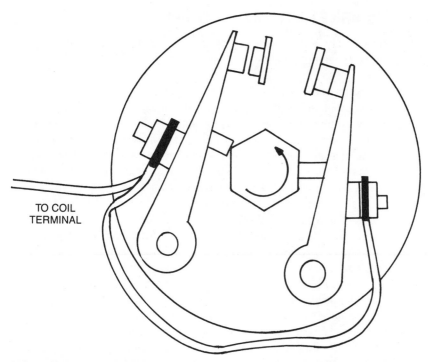

TO COIL
TERMINAL

Fig. 8-6. Dual-point ignition systems are useful with ignition systems that use breaker points. They permit a hotter spark for better ignition.

Both MSD and Carter make similar ping control systems. There might be others. The MSD system shown in Fig. 8-8 replaces the stock ignition module and has manual control of advance/retard. I believe Carter makes a similar manually controlled model plus an automatic model. The automatic model has a sensor that mounts on the engine block and "hears" any ping. Upon hearing the ping, electronic controls immediately retard spark enough to remove the ping. This model should work especially well on an engine with a turbocharger where ping can be very serious within a short period of time.

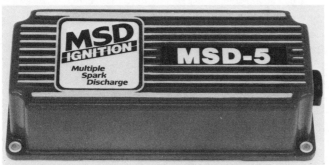

Fig. 8-7. This computer ignition system from MSD is a direct plug-in system for most cars except GM engines with HEI ignition. (Photo courtesy of MSD Ignition.)

Fig. 8-8. An adjustable timing control (ping control) from MSD replaces the OEM ignition module. (Photo courtesy of MSD Ignition.)

CUSTOM TUNING YOUR ENGINE

As I've said before, our vehicles come from the factory designed with lots of built-in compromises. The factory engineers have to make some assumptions about the way you drive without knowing anything about you. They also have to consider the governmental mandates on mileage and emissions. But one of the biggest variables they have to allow for is that no two engines are exactly alike. That's true even when they come off the same line.

It is impossible, in the manufacture of any product, to build to an absolute size. A cylinder, for example, may be designed to be 4.255 inches in diameter. But it is impossible to hold all cylinders to exactly that size. So tolerances are permitted. Some cylinders will be slightly smaller and some slightly larger. The same thing is true of the pistons that fit those cylinders. So what happens when one cylinder with maximum allowable size meets a piston with minimum allowable size? You're right, a relatively sloppy fit. Suppose that all eight cylinders in your engine happen to be that kind of fit. Now consider that the next engine down the line just happens to have the opposite set of tolerances. Which engine would you prefer?

Which engine did you get? I don't know either, and neither do the engineers. But they do know that somebody got both engines, and they both have to run reasonably well. So they prescribe a set of operating specifications that will work fairly well with all engines under a presumed set of operating conditions.

You can bet those conditions are not yours. You can also bet that your engine will run better if its operating specifications are fine-tuned for its set of tolerances. There is a fairly easy way to accomplish this fine-tuning and get yourself up to 10 percent more power with about the same increase in mileage. Legally, your mechanic can't do it. That's especially true if you go to the dealer. By law, mechanics are supposed to use the set of specifications determined by the factory. The idea is to assure that engine emissions meet the guidelines.

Well, there is almost nothing on my engine that meets the specifications, but every January it beats the emissions requirements by a wide margin. And my mileage has gone from 13 when I got the van to 18 with 125,000 miles on it.

IGNITION TIMING

Where to start? The easiest place to get better mileage and more power is with ignition timing. On all gasoline engines the timing is set for the spark to occur at some point just before the piston reaches top dead center on the compression stroke. The amount ahead of top dead center is called the advance. There are three types of advance that we have to work with.

Initial advance is the amount of advance in degrees that occurs when the engine is idling, before any other advance comes in. Initial advance has to be kept low so that the engine will idle well and start easily. As engine speed increases more advance is needed because things are happening more rapidly in the cylinders. It takes time for the flame front of the burning gasoline to move across the cylinder. The time is roughly the same whether the engine is idling at 800 rpm or running at 4,000 rpm. To make sure the flame front has time to do its thing the amount of advance increases with engine speed. That is called centrifugal or mechanical advance because it is controlled by a set of centrifugal weights in the distributor. As engine speed increases, the weights move out and deliver more ignition advance until the maximum designed advance occurs at somewhere over 3,200 rpm.

When an engine is operating under a heavy load, the combustion pressures inside the cylinder increase. That causes the flame front to travel faster. It can also cause some of the fuel/oxygen mixture to self-ignite if the pressure gets too high. That's one of the causes of ping. But when you are cruising down the road with a light load the combustion pressures are lower. What all that means is that an engine running at cruising speed under a light load can use even more ignition advance than one under a heavy load at the same speed.

To accommodate those differences engineers dial in the third kind of advance, vacuum advance. It works because under a light load the manifold vacuum will be higher than under a heavy load. There is a diaphragm device on the side of the distributor that reads the amount of vacuum (engine load) and controls the vacuum advance. What most mechanics seem not to realize is that the vacuum advance can be adjusted. On many Fords the vacuum advance device from the factory is adjustable with an allen wrench. The same is true of at least some Chrysler products. On GMs you have to buy an adjustable vacuum advance from your local speed shop. The one I have used is made by Crane Cams. Crane also makes an adjustable unit for Fords.

So, let's do it. You'll need a wrench that fits the hold-down bolt on your distributor, a $3/32$ allen wrench, and a golf tee. A timing light will help but isn't essential. Disconnect the hose from the vacuum advance, and plug it with the golf tee. Find a stretch of road that doesn't have much traffic, and note two markers about a tenth of a mile apart. If you have a Ford with automatic, put it in second gear. With other automatics just use drive. Line up with your first mark, and floor the accelerator and hold it there. Note the speed as accurately as you can when you pass the second mark. Did you hear any ping? A lot or very slight?

Go back to your first mark, and shut off the engine. If you heard no ping at all you want to give a bit more initial advance. If you heard a lot of ping you want to take some advance out. If the ping was very light, leave it alone.

To make adjustments, first determine the rotation of the inner workings of the distributor. The easy way is to make a fist with your right hand with your index finger extended. Place the bottom of your fist over the distributor with your index finger over the vacuum advance. If you can't, then use your left hand the same way. In either case, your index finger points the direction of more advance. Loosen the hold-down clamp. Carefully turn the distributor for greater or lesser advance according to what you determined you need. How much? That's the question. If you have a timing light, try two degrees. Without a light, try about a quarter of an inch of distributor movement. Tighten the clamp. Run your test again.

If you dialed in more advance, you're now looking for a slightly faster top speed at the second marker. If you still get no ping at all, go back to mark one and put in another two degrees of advance. Repeat the steps until you get ping. Then take out half of the last adjustment. If you have a timing light, check to see how much advance you now have and make a note of it. You might find that engine speed has increased enough that you will need to adjust idle speed on the carburetor.

Now plug the vacuum line back onto the vacuum advance unit. Go for a ride at 30 mph. Listen carefully for ping. If there is any ping, stop and remove the vacuum hose from the distributor. Insert a $3/32$ allen wrench in the neck where the hose was connected. Turn counterclockwise two turns, reinstall hose and drive again at 30. If ping continues, repeat until you get rid of it. If there was no ping on first trial, accelerate to 50. If there is any ping, repeat the steps mentioned above for adjusting.

If there is no ping, turn your allen wrench clockwise two turns and drive again at 50. Repeat until you get slight ping on acceleration at 50. Then adjust vacuum advance one turn counterclockwise. That should do it.

You might find that you get some ping when pulling a load. If so, just adjust the vacuum advance counterclockwise one turn at a time until you get rid of the ping. What you are doing is setting the load at which the vacuum advance retards timing to adjust for the load.

By following the steps outlined, you have tailored the ignition advance to your engine and the way you drive. You should get a noticeable increase in mileage and power unless you just happened to have the average engine and driving conditions every engineer dreams of but never expects.

If you buy the kit from Crane Cams for your GM engine, you will also find inside some springs for tailoring the centrifugal advance curve. Installation and adjustment are easy if you just follow the instructions.

SPARK PLUGS AND PLUG GAPS

Spark plugs have only one job to do, light the fire in the cylinders. Life should be so simple. Of course, life for a spark plug means doing your job 2,000 or more times a minute at temperature of over 3,000 degrees under fantastic pressures while getting no attention unless you foul up. Sounds like your job, Harry? Well, maybe you're a Champion. Sorry.

I've already mentioned the different types of plugs and how to make a selection among them. About the only thing left to consider is the plug gap, the space between the end of the center electrode and bottom of the side electrode. The size of this gap is important in more than one way. It's here, in this tiny space, that ignition of the fuel mixture takes place. The larger the gap that will work, the better. Engineers would like to use a gap of .100 inch. They can't, but they're getting closer.

The type of ignition system you have has an important bearing on the spark plug gap that is optimum for your car. Computer ignition systems can run very large gaps, as much as .80 inch. The right gap also depends on what you want from your engine. In general, a wider than normal gap gives an increase in mileage and a decrease in power. A less than normal gap usually has the opposite effect. The way to find the best gap for you and your car is to decide what you want. Are you after mileage or power? Then start with the stock-recommended gap. Carefully observe the results for 1,000 miles of driving. Run several careful power checks and record the results. Then increase the gap by .010 inch and repeat your tests. If the results are positive, increase another .010 inch and retest. Continue until you begin to get negative results; then go back to the previous setting. If your main concern is power, you might find that your best setting is somewhat less than the stock gap.

If you are working with a GM engine 1986 or older, replace the rotor with a heavy duty rotor. Standard GM rotors of those years tended to fail under the pressure of large spark plug gaps.

When adjusting spark plug gaps, be sure to keep the portion of the ground electrode perpendicular to the center electrode where it passes over. Filing this surface of the ground electrode flat is also worth doing.

9
CHAPTER

Carburetors, Injectors, and Manifolds

GASOLINE ENGINES DON'T RUN ON GASOLINE, BUT THEY WON'T RUN WITHOUT gasoline, either. All internal combustion engines, including gasoline engines, run on a very carefully balanced mixture of gasoline and air. Actually, they burn the oxygen in air, but it's more convenient to talk about gasoline and air mixtures. The device that has been most commonly used to control that gasoline/air mixture is the carburetor.

HOW CARBURETORS WORK, BRIEFLY

Fortunately for both you and me, having a complete knowledge of how carburetors work isn't necessary. As you can imagine, many books have been written on that subject alone. Here I'll just hit the high spots.

On four stroke engines, the kind used in almost all cars and trucks, the piston goes through four strokes to make one complete cycle. Obviously the cycle can begin anywhere, but it's easiest to think of it as beginning with the piston at the top of the cylinder. Follow Fig. 9-1 as I explain. As the piston moves down, an area of low pressure is created between the piston and the cylinder head. Air pressure outside the engine is continually at about 31 inches of Mercury. This outside pressure forces air into the cylinder to equalize the pressures inside and outside the cylinder. On the way in, it passes through the carburetor, which is nothing more than a fancy mixing device. As the air moves through the carburetor, it passes through the venturi. The venturi is nothing more than a specially shaped funnel that increases the velocity of the air. The venturi is named for an Italian physicist, Venturi, who discovered that when air flows through a restricted passage, flow is fastest and the pressure lowest at the point of greatest restriction. Figure 9-2 is a cross-section of the venturi tube in a simple car-

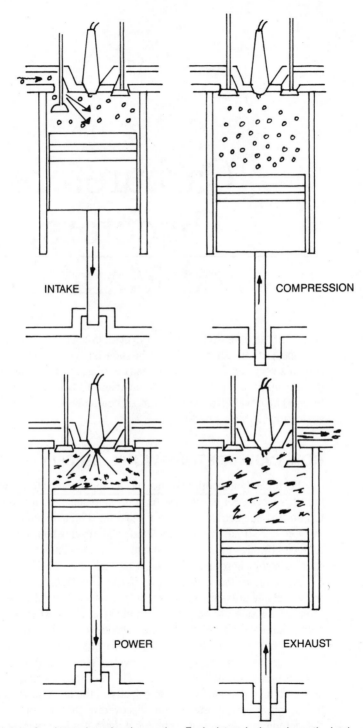

INTAKE

COMPRESSION

POWER

EXHAUST

Fig. 9-1. The four strokes of an internal combustion engine. Fuel mixture is drawn in on the intake stroke, compressed on the compression stroke, and burns on the power stroke. Exhaust gases are expelled on the exhaust stroke.

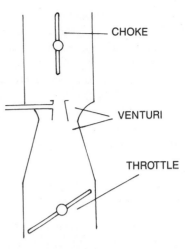

Fig. 9-2. Cross section of the throat or bore in a carburetor showing the choke valve, venturi, and throttle.

buretor. Since the pressure within the venturi is less than the pressure outside, the outside air pressure forces some fuel into the air stream passing through the venturi. Through a complicated series of internal air passages and jets, the proportion of air to fuel is kept between 12:1 and 17:1. The ideal, 14.7:1, is called the stoichiometric mixture and represents that mixture that exactly burns all of the fuel and oxygen.

As the load on the engine changes from idle to acceleration to cruise to heavy pulling, the ideal fuel/air mixture changes. By means of the internal passages and jets mentioned earlier, the mixture changes automatically in response to the load. Under a heavy load the mixture may be as low as 12.5:1. At idle the mixture may be as high as 17:1. The high speed and load mixtures are determined by fixed jets within the carburetor. Tailoring the mixture for specific engine and load requirements is done by partially disassembling the carburetor and changing the jets. On most carburetors, the idle mixture is adjustable. Until the mid-70s idle adjustment was easy; the idle adjustment screws were easy to find and could be turned through a wide range. Because of the demand to eliminate air pollutants from automobile exhausts, carburetors were changed to permit only limited idle mixture adjustments. Current idle mixture adjustment screws are sealed by a metal plug. It is necessary to break the plug in order to gain access to the adjustment screws.

Just downstream from the venturi is the throttle which consists of a movable plate. When the throttle is closed, very little air passes through and engine speed is low. Idle speed is controlled by a screw that holds the throttle slightly open. The wider the opening, the more fuel/air mixture passes through. Engine speed is controlled by variation in the throttle opening.

A similar movable plate, the choke, installed just upstream of the venturi, is used to aid in starting the engine. When the engine is cold, the fuel vaporizes less readily. A richer fuel/air mixture is required until the engine warms enough to vaporize the fuel. Closing the choke reduces the air pressure through the carburetor below normal, causing extra fuel to be drawn through the jets into the airstream.

From the carburetor the air/fuel mixture passes through the intake manifold to the individual cylinders. Intake manifolds consist of passages of varying size and with sufficient turns to reach all the cylinders. As the air/fuel mixture passes through these passages, some of the fuel tends to fall out of suspension. Also, the passages to the cylinders are not of equal length. Ideally, they would be, but constraints of manufacturing dictate that some will be longer than others. The result of varying lengths of passages and the fact that some fuel falls out of suspension is that not all cylinders receive the same quantity of air/fuel mixture or even the same mixture. Consequently, not all cylinders produce equal power.

WHY INJECTORS?

Fuel injectors are relatively simple devices that inject measured quantities of fuel either into the manifold or directly into the cylinder. Injectors have been around for many years. Diesel engines would not operate without injectors. The simplicity and accuracy of injectors have intrigued engineers for a long time. Many attempts to adapt them to gasoline engines were made with only limited success. The problem was that until very recently injectors were strictly mechanical in operation. Fuel was supplied to the injectors at high pressure. The actual injection was mechanically timed. Mechanical methods of timing injection did not permit the fine tuning necessary for gasoline engines.

With the emphasis on pollution control in the last decade, there have come increased demands for accuracy in controlling air/fuel mixtures. Fuel injectors always had a theoretical advantage. Control was the problem. Fortunately, computers became readily available at the same time. Engineers quickly turned to computers to handle the myriad precise measurements and controls needed to make injectors work for gasoline engines.

Because computers can read such things as engine speed, throttle position, load, operating temperatures, and ambient temperature at extremely high speeds for individual cylinders, they offered the possibility of achieving the kind of control necessary. On today's engines, computers read all these conditions and more. They also are able to control the injectors so that exact amounts of fuel are injected depending upon operating requirements.

Think of an injector as a precision squirt gun ready to squirt gasoline into the engine on demand. The computer senses the operating conditions of the engine, determines the precise amount of gasoline needed to meet those conditions, and pulls the trigger. The result is an engine that starts quickly, idles smoothly at all temperatures, develops more power than a carbureted engine, and gives better mileage.

TWO TYPES OF INJECTORS

There are at least two locations for fuel injectors. Some manufacturers have opted for placing one or two injectors together with a housing containing the throttle plate at the same location formerly used by the carburetor. This

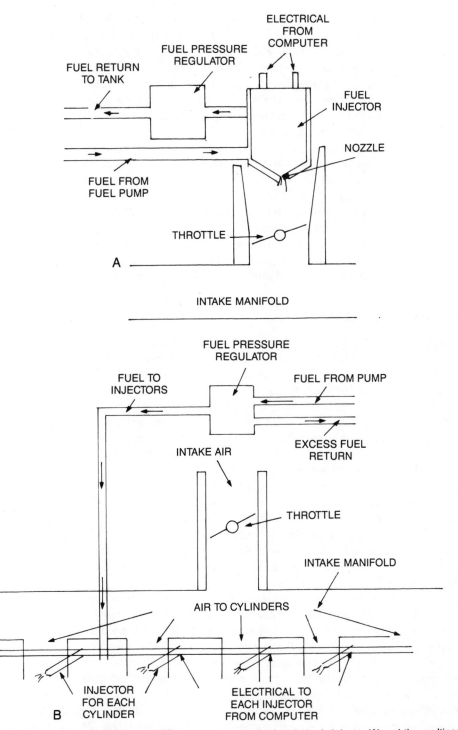

Fig. 9-3. These drawings show similarities and differences between the throttle-body injector (A) and the multiport injector system (B). Some manufacturers use two injectors in one throttle-body to give results similar to a two-barrel carburetor.

type of injector is called a throttle-body injector. Throttle-body injectors inject a continuous stream of fuel with the amount being determined by the computer. In effect, the throttle-body injector is an electronically controlled carburetor without all the jets and air passages. It offers more precise fuel control than a carburetor, but it does have one serious handicap. It still sits in the same place formerly occupied by the carburetor, and the air/fuel mixture still traverses the intake manifold passages. The fuel still tends to drop out of suspension, and there are still differences between cylinders.

To supply even more accurate fuel control and eliminate the problems associated with fuel suspension in the manifold, some manufacturers have gone to the multiport injection system. Multiport injection systems locate an injector at the end of the manifold just outside each cylinder. Only air passes through the manifold. Each cylinder has its own injector. All manifold passages can be the same length. There are no differences in amounts of fuel among the cylinders. The result is a smoother running engine that develops optimum power and economy. Of course, having additional injectors increases the cost, but the results seem to be worthwhile. Figure 9-3 illustrates the two injector systems.

CUSTOM IGNITION CHIPS

To supply the information needed for the injectors, computers have become an integral part of modern engines. Without the computer the myriad bits of information and the precise control needed would not be possible. But fuel control is not the only area where the computer is being used. Today's sophisticated engines also require precision control of the engine ignition. Earlier I mentioned that most engines now use some form of computer ignition system. These two computer systems, fuel control and ignition control, work together to assure that the engine operates under optimum conditions. Fuel is precisely measured and injected at the instant needed. Ignition is timed and tailored for the most efficient possible fuel burn. It would appear that we have the best of all possible engine operating conditions. Why would anyone want more?

There are reasons. One is the natural curiosity of many owners who wonder if they couldn't make the engine run a bit better. Another reason is that, in spite of all the computer sophistication, the engineers still have to make some assumptions about operating conditions and driving styles. Their assumptions are probably different from your conditions.

With almost total electronic control, tuning an engine is vastly more difficult than it used to be. Fuel injectors don't permit easy modification. The computer isn't readily reprogrammed. Changing to a different manifold is not the simple task it once was. About the only thing that's left is to work with the computer. While we can't reprogram the whole computer, we can substitute new chips for old ones in some instances. Within the computer there are numerous modules called chips. Each chip contains instructions for the engine. One might control the ignition timing. Another controls the quantity of fuel injected. By installing custom chips, it is possible to make small changes in the engine operation. At the time of writing, power chips are only available for certain models of General

Motors engines. GM uses computers with plug-in chips. Most other manufacturers use chips that are soldered in. It is probable that chips for soldered-in computers will eventually be available.

TUNING YOUR CARBURETOR

It seems ironic to talk about carburetors after all the high tech discussion of injectors and computers, but the fact remains that there are several million cars and trucks out there with carburetors. It seems probable that there will be carbureted engines around for a long, long time. There are even owners of fuel injected, computer controlled engines who are converting to carburetors. Why?

Well, carburetors have been around since the beginning of gasoline engines. There are millions of mechanics who are comfortable with them and who know very little about injectors and computers. Repairing injectors and computers requires expensive and sophisticated equipment that most of us can't afford. And there are many engineers who believe that carburetors can be at least equal to injectors and computers. I won't get into the argument of which is better, but there is no argument about which is easier to work with and modify.

One of the most popular modifications to older engines is the replacement or modification of the carburetor. There is a mystique about carburetors that cannot be ignored. Thousands of owners are convinced that they could double the horsepower of their engines if they could just find the right carburetor. Thousands more are equally certain that somewhere there is a carburetor that will double their mileage. Carburetor replacement is simple and relatively inexpensive. New carburetors of all sizes abound, and old carburetors of just as many sizes are available at the salvage yard. Just take your pick and bolt it on.

SELECTING A REPLACEMENT CARBURETOR

But which one? Most advertising material from carburetor manufacturers stresses either horsepower or fuel economy with the larger emphasis on power. Carburetors are rated by their ability to flow a given volume of air per minute. Because gasoline engines run on air, mixed with a little gasoline, it would seem that the more air an engine gets in, the more power it puts out. Within limits, that is true, but the problem is not that simple. To use more air the engine has to run faster and have a camshaft and manifold and exhaust system designed for high speed. Such an engine is worthless at low speed. Many of them won't even run at the speeds we can operate on the highway. Many racing engines idle at more than 3,000 rpm.

A carburetor that will flow 700 cubic feet per minute (cfm) may be perfect for a racing engine and worthless for a street engine. How do you determine the right size carburetor for a street engine?

There is a formula that is helpful, but first there is more theory. The fuel intake characteristics that develop low speed torque are vastly different from the ones that develop maximum horsepower. Horsepower depends on time and distance. Another way of saying that is the horsepower depends on speed.

Torque is just force. Torque is what gives us the kick in the pants when we press the accelerator. Torque climbs the hill. Horsepower determines how quickly those things happen. Horsepower depends on torque. You can have torque without horsepower, but you can't have horsepower without torque. We need both, of course, but we need torque at low engine speeds more than we need horsepower at high engine speeds.

An engine can be tuned to develop maximum torque at almost any speed you choose. Most racers want it at 3,500 to 5,000 rpm. An engine designed for maximum torque at those speeds will hardly run at 2,000 rpm. Street autos are usually geared for an engine speed of 2,500 to 3,500 on the highway. Most of us want our engines to idle fairly smoothly at 800 to 1,000 rpm and pull powerfully from idle up to highway speed. That kind of operation requires an engine that develops maximum torque near 2,500 rpm and a totally different carburetor from the one the racer will use.

A carburetor designed for low-speed torque will have small barrels to keep the air/fuel mixture moving at high speed through the carburetor and manifold. Such a carburetor will give a smooth idle, good economy, and lots of low-speed power. But it will run out of capacity at high speed. High speed requires a larger barrel. A compromise that has been popular for at least two decades is the multibarrel carburetor. Four-barrel carburetors, popular on V-8s, have two small barrels for idle and most cruising, and two larger barrels for high speed and maximum power running. Smaller engines frequently use a two-barrel carburetor with one small and one large barrel for the same purpose. The larger barrels only open when the engine is under full load and operating at 2,800 to 3,000 rpm. These carburetors offer an excellent compromise between maximum torque at low speed and near maximum power at high speed.

But which one and what size? That's about like asking what kind of wife or husband you should have. Personal driving requirements are the big variable. One thing you can be fairly certain about, however, is that the carburetor that came from the factory is probably larger than you need. A good way to determine the size carburetor you need is to use the formula Carb Size = (Engine Displacement × Max. RPM) / 3,456. That gives the volume of air/fuel mixture the engine would use at that speed if it operated at 100 percent volumetric efficiency. Since the engine that operates at 100 percent volumetric efficiency is rare, multiply the results by .80. For an example, assume you have a Chevy 350 and don't expect to run it over 3,500 rpm. Multiply 350 by 3,500, divide by 3,456, and multiply the result by .80. The formula suggests that a carburetor that flows 283 cfm would be about right. You won't find one that size. Look for a 350 cfm carb. You can bet that the one you have is larger. Why? Well, the manufacturer believes that horsepower sells cars. He tries to get the maximum horsepower figure that will usually be developed at about 4,500 rpm. So he puts on a big carburetor to get that speed and power. Then he builds in a cushion. That 350 engine probably came from the factory with a 600 cfm carburetor. That's too big for best street performance.

Performance shops have lots of carburetors for sale. Try and find one near the size you have determined you need with vacuum operated secondaries. The secondaries are the second set of barrels for high speed and power. If they are vacuum operated, they won't open until your engine gets to high speed under a load. Be sure the carb you get will fit the manifold you're using. Use the same approach if you go to the salvage yard. Look for a carburetor from an engine smaller than yours. Fortunately, there are families of carburetors with standard bases.

Whatever carburetor you get might need to have the main jets changed. That's a trial and error operation. A good carburetor mechanic can be very helpful. You can do it yourself if you're careful and take the time to learn how to read your plugs. Jets that are too large will give a soft, black, sooty coating to the plugs. Plugs that are too small will leave the plugs looking burned with tiny blisters. The car will also seem sluggish, as if it's not getting enough gas. It isn't. Running too lean can result in burned valves. It's better to err slightly on the side of too rich.

MANIFOLDS AND OTHER MAGIC

The intake manifold fits between the carburetor and the engine head. Its function is to carry the air/fuel mixture to the combustion chambers, the cylinders. The intake manifold on a one cylinder engine is simple; it's one tube. Two cylinders are just about as simple. After that the situation gets complicated. All the passages, called runners, in a manifold should be exactly the same length and shape. Obviously, that's impossible with multicylinder engines.

I've already mentioned the problem with fuel fallout in the manifold. It's a serious problem. OEM manifolds are all compromises. They could be better, but cost becomes a difficulty. Making a better manifold might increase the unit cost only $30, but a company's accountants keep multiplying that $30 by 1,000,000 or so. The result is a less expensive and less efficient manifold. Another result is the vast array of aftermarket manifolds of all descriptions. Edelbrock, just one of several manufacturers of specialty manifolds, offers eight manifolds for the small-block Chevy engines. The advertising material on all of them is attractive and offers huge increases in power. What's a guy to do?

The first thing to do is decide what you want out of your engine. Many of the same principles apply here that applied to the selection of a carburetor. This is another place where bigger is definitely not better. Be honest with yourself about engine speeds. Sure, we all like to think about an engine roaring at 6,500 rpm, but we don't run them that way, at least we don't on the street.

That high-rise manifold illustrated in Fig. 9-4 with the carburetor perched nearly a foot above the stock location may look great, but the fact is it runs pretty sour on the street. High-rise manifolds were designed for racing, not for the street. Choosing the wrong manifold will surely result in an engine that might look great standing at the curb, but it won't look quite so fine lurching down the street. Be brutal with yourself. Fortunately, most manifold builders are honest at telling you the rpm range each manifold was designed for. Believe them.

Fig. 9-4. This high-rise manifold looks great and is fine for racing, but it doesn't work well on a street machine. (Photo courtesy of Weiand Automotive.)

AIR CLEANERS AREN'T CREATED EQUAL

When I was a teenager the rage was to remove the air cleaner and run with the carburetor sitting out there in the open. Naive as we were, we thought that removing the restriction of the air cleaner was a sure way to get more power. We were probably right—for a few miles. That air cleaner was important and we found it out when the top rings on the pistons went out from handling too much dirt. The air cleaner is another component of the engine that gets little respect.

An air cleaner is an air cleaner, right? Unless it's chromed, of course. Then it becomes a shiny, chrome air cleaner. But who cares? Well, you should. Just remember that your 350-cubic-inch engine ingests over 15,000 cubic feet of air per hour of highway driving. Then think about all the junk that's in that air. Do you really want that stuff in your engine? Most of it's not only dirty, but also abrasive, like sandpaper. Unless you had changed the air cleaner on an engine after 20,000 miles or so, you wouldn't believe some of the crud that found its way to the top of your carburetor. I haven't found a bird there yet, but I have found quantities of sand and dust, straw, and insects as large as butterflies. A small bird wouldn't greatly surprise me.

Okay, you're convinced, but aren't all air cleaners alike? No way. They look similar, and they're made of similar materials. But the White House is made out of materials similar to those used in the privy back on the farm. There is a subtle difference.

Most air filters built today use folded paper as the filtering element. Some add other filtering material and some use a wire mesh as a supporting member. At least one manufacturer adds an oiled foam strip surrounding the paper. Figure 9-5 shows a typical air filter. Theoretically, all do the same job. In practice, there are differences. In one test of eight different brand air filters, all of the same size, one filter showed the ability to flow 825 cubic feet of air per minute while another flowed only 411 cfm. The others were somewhere between the two. Clearly, there are differences among air filters. K & N is a reusable filter. That is, after being used for several thousand miles it can be washed, reoiled, and placed back in service. All others are intended to be used and thrown away. The K & N costs significantly more. Is it worth it? Well, the K & N was the filter that flowed 825 cfm. The second best in the test flowed 601 cfm. You be the judge.

There are some things in life where buying the less expensive product is acceptable. It doesn't make a lot of difference which shoestring you buy for your walking shoes. I expect my engines to last for 150,000 miles before major repair. That repair might cost $2,000. If I can get 150,000 miles rather than 50,000 miles by changing the air filter five times, it makes sense to me to change it. It also makes sense to me to use the best to protect my investment.

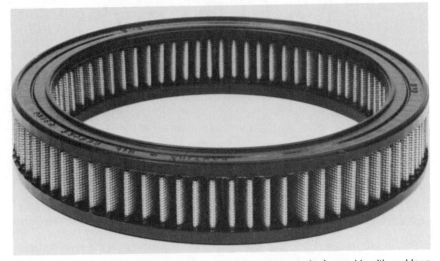

Fig. 9-5. An air cleaner such as this one is essential to your engine's good health and long life. (Photo courtesy of K & N Filters.)

CHAPTER

Mufflers and Exhaust Systems

THERE ARE TWO LAWS OF EXHAUST SYSTEMS. THE FIRST IS, "WHAT GOES IN MUST come out." The second law is, "If you don't empty it, you can't fill it." An understanding of both of these laws is essential to getting maximum performance from your engine. Let's look at them in turn.

EXCESS BACK PRESSURE CUTS POWER

You see, in Fig. 10-1, that an engine develops power on the power stroke. The rapidly burning fuel/air mixture expands with tremendous force, pushing the piston down. All the torque and all the power that the engine develops are right here, in the power stroke. If the cylinder is successful in being completely filled with an air/fuel mixture on the intake stroke, the engine can develop all the torque of which it is capable on this power stroke.

But the end product of the combustion process is three things: pressure on the piston, excess heat absorbed by the engine parts, and a mass of burned gases that have no further use. Not only do these burned gases have no further use; they are excess baggage that must be gotten out of the way. As long as those gases (or any part of them) remain in the cylinder, the cylinder cannot receive a full charge of fresh air/fuel mixture. To discharge the gases, the piston completes its cycle on the exhaust stroke with the intake valve closed and the exhaust valve open. The objective is to push all the burned gases out the exhaust valve and away from the engine.

Those gases are still very hot. Releasing them directly into the air would burn some of the objects in the immediate area. Those objects are such things as other engine parts, wiring, body panels, fuel lines, perhaps your own body

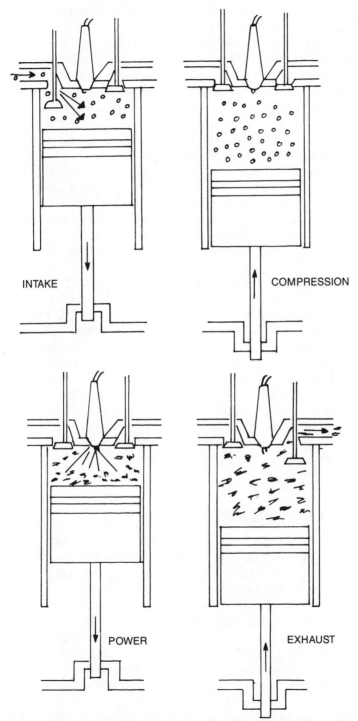

INTAKE

COMPRESSION

POWER

EXHAUST

Fig. 10-1. We saw this before when we were discussing carburetors. What goes into an engine must get out. On the exhaust stroke the rising piston pushes the burned gases out into the exhaust system.

parts. Releasing the gases directly would also create quite a lot of noise and gain the attention of various persons who object to your loud noises.

So, engine designers collect the exhaust gases in a chamber that is connected to each of the exhaust ports from the cylinders. The chamber is called the exhaust manifold and consists of a short passage from each of the cylinders, a large chamber collecting the gases from all the cylinders, and another passage connecting to a pipe that carries the gases to a safe disposal area. Unfortunately, the gases are still noisy, so the exhaust pipe connects to a device called a muffler to alter the noises and make them more acceptable. Finally, another pipe called the tail pipe carries the now subdued gases away.

It all sounds complicated when you think about it, and it is. Exhaust systems appear to be relatively simple systems that serve as a sort of garbage system for burned gases. What could be complicated or interesting about that?

Well, for openers, every piece of the exhaust system does its bit to slow down the passage of exhaust gases. That means that some pressure is exerted toward not letting all the gases escape. Back to the second law of exhausts: "If you don't empty it, you can't fill it."

As an example, suppose you're given a 3-gallon bucket and told to carry six gallons of water to that tank over there. You fill the bucket with three gallons, pour two gallons into the tank, and go back to the pump. This time there is a gallon still in the bucket. You can only add two more gallons. If you don't get smart and empty the bucket completely into the tank, you're going to make more than the minimum of two trips to get six gallons of water. What, you say, does that have to do with exhaust systems and engines?

If the exhaust system is restrictive, and all of them are to some extent, then the cylinder can never be filled completely with a fresh cylinder of air/fuel. That 45-cubic-inch cylinder becomes a 35 incher. Instead of a 360-inch engine, you have a 280. On the intake stroke the cylinder already holds 10 cubic inches of burned gases, so it takes in only 35 cubic inches rather than the 45 you hoped for. Tough.

SINGLES, DUALS, AND HEADERS

Can you do anything about it? Sure, that's why I'm writing this book! One of the first things to go should be the exhaust manifold. A problem with manifolds is the very short stacks from the exhaust ports to the main chamber. When burning gases leave the exhaust port they begin to set up shock waves that travel back and forth through the gas column. If the column is short, as in the typical manifold, the waves become confused and might add their energy in the wrong direction. They might even add pressure against the gases trying to escape from one of the other exhaust ports. It's true that some manifolds do a pretty good job of getting the gases out, but the good ones are few and far between. It's better to assume that yours is one of the poor ones, and replace it with a header.

Not just any header will do. Headers became popular many years ago when it was popular to build for maximum power at high engine speeds. Sound familiar? Some of the header designers haven't gotten off that kick. Also, some of them build their headers from lightweight tubing. Exhaust gases are very hot. Lightweight tubing doesn't last very long. Replacing a set of burned-out headers is expensive and time-consuming. Insist on heavyweight tubing.

As for size, we're back to some of the same theory used with carburetors. Bigger is not always better. Big tubing is great for removing huge amounts of burned gases from big, high-speed engines. But big tubing tends to mess up the low-speed torque characteristics of the engine. We are building for maximum torque at realistic engine speeds. That calls for smaller tubing than many header builders want to work with. It's your engine; insist on getting what you want. Four- and six-cylinder engines should have headers with tubing no larger than 1⅝ inches, and 1½ inches would be preferred. Larger engines up to about 400 inches can use 1¾ inch tubing. The monster 440s, 454s, and 460s can use 2-inch tubing. Collector cones can be 2¼ inches tapering to an exhaust pipe about ¼ inch larger than the header tubes. A crossover pipe between the two banks should be installed following the collectors. Then we have to stop and plan some more.

Since shortly after the government became interested in our physical welfare as it is affected by air pollution, we have had something called a catalytic converter attached to our exhaust systems. The converter contains a catalyst, usually a compound of platinum, that causes a further chemical reaction in the exhaust gases as they pass through the converter. The idea is to clean the exhaust gases of remaining hydrocarbons and other noxious materials. Unfortunately, catalytic converters have achieved a bad reputation for restricting the flow of exhaust gases. Also unfortunately, removing them from the system is illegal.

If your car or truck has an engine that is certified for use of unleaded gas and a catalytic converter, you have two options in building your exhaust system. You can remove the offending converter and take your chances with the government. Or you can install a converter of ample size in each exhaust pipe downstream from the crossover pipe. If you have a dual-exhaust system you are legally required to have two converters. Converters are not cheap, but neither are fines for violating the law. You can take some consolation in the fact that having two converters, each of at least the size that supposedly handles the whole system, will inflict less restriction than will the single system.

As to removing the converter, I have some very definite thoughts. I live in a part of Wisconsin that requires annual emissions testing. If you can pass the test, no one inspects your vehicle to see if all systems are intact. My van is sufficiently well-tuned to pass the test every year without the converter. Technically, I am legal because I have replaced the old engine with a larger one that is certified without the use of the converter.

But my van is still tested as if it had the original engine and must pass the emissions test for the original engine equipped with a converter. With one eye on the air that I and others must breathe, I still burn unleaded fuel 90 percent of the time. The only exception is when I am pulling our travel trailer. Then I burn regular for the small quantity of lead and its beneficial effect on engine valves under heavy duty use. That's information for you to use any way you choose.

Downstream of the converters you should install mufflers. Since you have gone to the expense of building a quality exhaust system, it makes no sense to skimp here. The best would probably be twin glasspacks of good quality about 40 inches long for the larger engines. Smaller engines, fours and V-6s, would probably be happy with 30-inch glasspacks. Cores should be the same diameter as the rest of the pipe you have been using, slightly larger than the headers. Twin glasspacks with a crossover tube in front are usually not too loud and they are effectively low-restrictive. A second choice would be the so-called turbo mufflers. These mufflers are usually quite low in restriction but somewhat noisy. I love them, but my wife found them a bit uncomfortable. Another of life's compromises.

There's usually one more pipe, the tail pipe that extends from the rear of the muffler to a convenient dumping area. The location of the tail pipe does require some planning. The gases coming out of the pipes are not exactly healthful. One of the gases is likely to be CO, carbon monoxide. CO does nasty things to living organisms. It is an odorless gas that is absorbed into the blood stream, gives you a headache, makes you sleepy, and makes you dead. Carbon monoxide is not to be fooled around with. The problem is that ventilation in many cars is very haphazardly planned. Backdrafts often exist, pulling air from around the rear and bottom of the car into the interior. This can be through rear windows or rust holes in the underpan or along the bottoms of the doors.

It's essential for the tail pipes to terminate in a location that will prevent exhaust gases from being drawn back into the car. Terminating the pipes even with the rear bumper and with a downward curve usually works well on sedans and coupes. On wagons and trucks, that location is not the best. Vehicles with blunt rear ends, such as wagons and trucks, tend to create powerful backdrafts swirling up from the underside of the rear of the vehicle. If there are any leaks in the body structure near the rear or if the rear window of a wagon is open, the result can be large quantities of exhaust gas drawn into the vehicle. Not good at all. For these types of vehicles I prefer terminating the tail pipes just in front or just behind the rear wheels with the ends of the pipes aimed to the side and down and reaching the outer edge of the body. That has worked well for me in keeping exhaust gases out of the passenger compartments.

COMPROMISES

Clearly, not all of us can do all the things we might like to do in modifying our vehicles. What portions of the exhaust system can be left to a later time? Does it have to be done all at once?

Probably the largest single expense in the custom exhaust system is the headers. Are they essential? No. An exhaust system can be improved at minimal expense by keeping the stock manifolds and building a dual system from there. The suggested sizes of tubing are still pertinent. With the cooperation of your friendly muffler shop, you can build a very satisfactory dual system from the stock manifolds. If you need to cut expense even more, use two stock mufflers. Certainly, two mufflers are better than one. With stock mufflers, you can probably forgo the crossover pipe, although it would be a rather minor expense. Changing the stock mufflers to glasspacks or turbos at a later date would give you a chance to update the system in stages.

I have no money saving suggestions for the second catalytic converter. I know that you can buy a used converter from some salvage yards. What I don't know is the condition of those converters. A driver can plug a converter with only a few tanks of leaded gasoline. You don't want his converter. Perhaps buying a converter from a low-mileage wreck that otherwise appears to have been well maintained would be safe. You take your chances.

11
CHAPTER

Cut the Drag

ONE OBVIOUS BUT OFTEN OVERLOOKED FACTOR IN PERFORMANCE IS THAT A VEHI-
cle will perform better if it isn't dragging something along with it. Unless pulling
a trailer is necessary to the mission of the trip, very few drivers will pull one. It
just makes no sense to hang on another 1,000 lbs. of drag. But every manufacturer and lots of owners build extra drag into their cars.

AIR TURBULENCE AND THE MODERN CAR

Back in the early 1900s the shape of a car was not very important. The
whole idea of a powered vehicle was new. Getting rid of the horse was such an
innovation that no one cared about efficiency. Of course the high speeds of the
day were under 20 miles per hour, well under. Aerodynamic drag was not a term
in every engineer's lunch conversation. With minor and rare exceptions, the situation didn't change until the mid-30s. If you look back at some of the designs of
luxury cars of the 20s, it would be easy to assume that the flowing lines of
fenders and rear ends of cars were a nod to the laws of aerodynamics. Flatly
denying that engineers of those days were aware of aerodynamic drag would be
unfair, but it is more likely that the flowing lines were due more to styling than
to engineering innovation.

Chrysler Corporation seems to have been the first to recognize that vehicles could be made to move more easily through the air if the vehicle shapes
were rounded. Their Airflow designs of the mid-30s were outrageously innova-
tive for their time. Sales figures showed that the public didn't care for innova-
tions in that direction. The fact that the cars also suffered from terminal
ugliness didn't help. The public just was not ready for teardrop-shaped cars.
Why worry about streamlined cars when the cost of gasoline was 15 cents a gal-

lon and 50 miles per hour was an exhilarating speed? Anyway, it was commonly understood that streamlining has no effect at speeds under about 75 mph. As we shall see, this was another case where what was commonly understood to be true was wrong.

World War II made a lot of changes in our lives. One way the war affected automobiles was in making the public more aware of the relationship between shape and speed. Airplanes had been around for decades, but World War II forced a quantum leap in their engineering. Most countries' air forces were barely out of the bi-wing era when the war began. The necessity for speed and the efficiency that made it possible to fly long distances forced an awareness of streamlining. At the beginning of the war 150 mph was considered high speed flying. Within five years, aircraft speeds were approaching 500 mph. In order to make those speeds possible it was necessary to reshape the airplane.

The lessons were not lost on those citizens destined to keep both feet on the ground. The shapes of cars began to copy the shapes of airplanes. Apparent streamlining became a selling point that automobile stylists could not pass up. The fact that much of the streamlining was more apparent than real was irrelevant to both the designers and the buying public. Cars had to look fast.

Whatever the reasons for the new shapes, there was a significant improvement in automotive aerodynamics. Somewhere along the way, however, even the reasons were lost. Nonfunctional fins, windshield sun visors, bulbous headlights and bumper ornaments, overly wide bodies—these and more styling appurtenances became the norm. But who cared? Gasoline was absurdly cheap and engines were so large that brute force sufficient to overcome almost any amount of drag was inexpensive. Streamlining was a styling word, not an engineering term.

Then came the infamous energy crunch. Gasoline prices soared to over $1.50 a gallon and gave every appearance of being headed for $2.00. Suddenly the people of at least some parts of the world realized that gasoline and its petroleum source were not available in infinite supply. The government stepped in with CAFE, the mandated corporate mileage averages, and automotive aerodynamics became important.

But what about that common understanding that aerodynamics was unimportant at speeds below 75 mph? With speed limits legally set at the double nickel, why worry about aerodynamics? Engineers frantically looking for every possible way to meet the mandated mileage figures took another look at aerodynamics. What they knew but everyone had forgotten in the halcyon days of the 50s and 60s was that aerodynamic drag increased as the cube of velocity and it made no difference where that velocity base was. Increasing velocity from 20 mph to 60 mph increased the drag not 3 times but 27 times. Put another way, it takes 27 times as much power to overcome a given amount of drag at 60 mph as it takes at 20 mph. Power means fuel. Now the engineers had peoples' attention. It is probably safe to say that few cars have been released for production since 1982 that the designer didn't first subject to a wind tunnel to determine their drag.

FRONTAL AREA AND DRAG

What determines the aerodynamic drag of a vehicle? Shape, size, and speed. Except to understand that increasing speed increases drag and fuel consumption, let's ignore speed for now. The main factor in size of a vehicle, as it affects drag, is frontal area. How much air does it push aside as it moves through the air? If a car were a box, figuring the frontal area would be easy: just multiply the width by the height. The older models made it simple, but modern cars are not just boxes. The body lines undulate in and out both vertically and from front to rear. From our standpoint, there isn't a lot we can do about the frontal area other than select a car that is reasonable in frontal size. Remember the General Motors cars of the early 70s? They had nearly 15 inches of space on either side between the outer shoulders of the passengers and the outer skin of the car. That was a classic example of frontal area gone berserk. Select a model with as little wasted frontal area as possible.

The shape of our automobiles is something we can work with. Try to imagine a car shaped like a classic teardrop, bluntly rounded in front and tapering to a point in the rear. That's the shape we're after. Notice anything hanging out on our imaginary teardrop? That's a good place to start.

DISPLACING AIR REQUIRES ENERGY

Whenever an object moves through a fluid such as air, the air is displaced. Displacing the air requires energy, power. As the object moves, the air is pushed out of the way, flows over the object, and returns to its approximate former position. The more smoothly the airflow takes place, the less power is required. How can you tell if the air is being displaced smoothly? Listen to it. Air that is not displaced smoothly assumes a turbulent flow. The molecules of air tumble around and vibrate. We hear the vibration as noise. If you can hear a roaring, even slight, as an object moves through the air, you can be sure you are listening to the results of turbulent flow.

Listen to the air roar as it passes your side mirrors. Hear it whistle through cracks around window and door seals. Notice noise as the wind is forced around hood ornaments, radio antennas, and windshield sun visors. Anything that protrudes from the smooth shape of the automobile body creates turbulent flow. Some protrusions blend in better than others and create less turbulence. The new external mirrors that blend in with the body are better than the older ones that sprout from stalks.

AIR DAMS

One area of turbulence that lends itself to a relatively easy cure is the car's underside. Air that is met head on by the car is forced mostly up and over or down and under. A small amount goes around the sides, but that will be dealt with later. The portion that goes up and over meets with little resistance in the early part of its trip unless you have installed a sun visor. The story is a bit different for the portion that goes down and under. To put it bluntly, that's a rough trip.

Unlike the portion that goes up and over, the air that goes under has no room to spread out. It is compressed into the relatively small space between the car body and the pavement. After being compressed, the air is forced around front end suspension parts, the engine pan, the transmission, exhaust system, drive shaft, various body bumps and appendages, the frame members, differential, rear wheels, wheel wells, gas tank, more brakes, and the rear bumper. No wonder it complains with lots of noise at all the turbulence. Underbody turbulence is possibly the largest single loss of aerodynamics in most cars.

As if the turbulence were not enough, the compressed air does what all compressed air does; it tries to reduce the compression by escaping. One way it tries to reduce the compression is by lifting the car. If you could measure the apparent weight of the car on the pavement at high speed, you would discover a significant weight loss. To put it differently, the tires don't press as hard against the pavement. Part of your precious traction has gone up in turbulence. The greater the speed, the greater this traction loss. At some point the car will literally lift off. Fortunately, most cars can never reach lift off speed, but the loss of traction is significant. The use of spoilers over the rear end of race cars is one attempt to regain some of the traction. Rear spoilers have become popular styling devices among car owners who emulate racers.

Another device for alleviating underbody turbulence is the front end air dam. The dams, made of fiberglass or some soft plastic, reach from the bottom of the bumper to near the pavement with the ends curving back to smooth the flow of air around the sides. By decreasing the amount of air that is forced under the car, the dams reduce the underbody turbulence and pressure. Noise is decreased, incipient lift-off is lessened, and drag is reduced. There is evidence that installing front air dams increases fuel mileage. You can increase the effectiveness of the dams by extending the curved ends backward along the rocker panels to the rear end. Of course, that poses some problems with decreased clearance that may reduce the value of the extensions.

Air dams can cause other problems. The front brakes are particularly susceptible to heat because they do the major part of the braking. Without an air dam there is ample air flowing over the brakes to cool them. An air dam restricts the flow of air—exactly what it is intended to do—and the brakes can suffer. Some owners compensate by building ducts to carry cooling air to the brakes and/or by installing wheels that pull air over the brakes and out through the wheels. The benefit of the wheels seems questionable, but properly designed ducts can result in brakes that are more effectively cooled than they were before the dam was installed. If you install a front air dam, by all means add cooling ducts to the brakes.

Some manufacturers are considering full underpans for the next generation of new cars. Made of plastic or aluminum, the underpans will smooth the passage of air under the car but, without some very careful engineering, will not eliminate the lift-off effect. If you try this yourself, be aware that there are some serious problems to be considered. The air that cools the engine must be released somewhere or the engine compartment becomes overheated and the engine will be damaged. Currently, most of the engine heat is released under the car's body. There is also a conduit of very hot air, the exhaust system, that traverses this underbody area. Part of the exhaust system is the catalytic converter. Under some circumstances, the converter runs almost red hot. Confining the hot air from the converter and exhaust pipes would be a very serious mistake. Just consider the effect it would have on the gasoline tank which is also part of the underbody environment.

SPOILERS

Spoilers were originally devices installed on the rear of racers to counteract some of the lift generated by the underbody air pressure. In a short time, all the would-be racers had to have them on their Mustangs, Camaros, and 'Birds. The aftermarket obliged as they always will when there is a market. Shortly the manufacturers of the sporty cars installed spoilers at the factory. Finding a sporty car without spoilers now would be about the same as finding Diogenes' honest man. Figure 11-1 is an example of a car with a rear spoiler.

How effective are these spoilers? That depends on what you want them to do. Seriously, how many owners of the above cars ever reach near lift-off speed other than in their heads? The reason for spoilers is style and nothing else, but they do have an effect, a negative effect. Air that is displaced up and over the

Fig. 11-1. The spoiler on this Firebird is more for looks than for aerodynamic efficiency. It likely produces a small negative effect, but it does look sharp.

car tries to follow the lines of the body as closely as possible and assume its former location as the car passes. When that air reaches the spoiler it is given an upward push. The result is more turbulence. Look under a rear spoiler on a car that has been driven where there is some dust. You will find a thick layer of dust forced there by the turbulence. Other than the psychological effect of the spoiler, the chief effect is a decrease in fuel mileage.

There is another type of spoiler that does have a positive effect on mileage. Station wagons, vans, and pickups are notorious for the dust and grime they accumulate on the rear end. This is caused by the low pressure area created as the vehicle passes through the air. As mentioned earlier, the air goes up and over, down and under, or around the vehicle and tries to assume its former location at the rear. But it can't. The curves of vans, wagons, and trucks are just too abrupt. Air has little mass, but it does have some. The laws of inertia apply to that mass. As vehicle speed increases, the inertia of the air becomes greater and the air finds it impossible to flow smoothly over the rear surfaces of the vehicle. The result is an area of low pressure at the rear of the vehicle. Dust and grime are "pulled" into this low pressure area and settle on the rear surfaces of the vehicle.

Some manufacturers of station wagons recognized the problem and built a small wing just above the rear, top corner of the wagon. See Fig. 11-2. The wing is shaped so as to force some of the air coming over the top to move across the rear surface of the wagon. Wagons with these wings are much freer of dirt and grime that are wagons without the wings. Designing and installing a small wing to the rear of other wagons, vans, and pickups would not be too difficult. Because of the blunt rear surfaces of many cars, the addition of such a wing would help them, too. The result would be not only a cleaner vehicle, but an increase in fuel mileage.

Fig. 11-2. The spoiler on this utility vehicle is set at an angle that forces some of the air down over the rear. The result is an improvement in airflow, some mileage improvement, and a cleaner tailgate.

MIRRORS, SQUIRREL TAILS, AND CANOES

Mirrors, squirrel tails, and canoes make strange bedfellows. To the list I should add sun visors, radio antennas, flags, and plastic foam balls. These, and others, are the sort of things that owners hang on their cars. Mirrors of some sort are a must. The driver who doesn't keep track of what is behind him is headed for an expensive education. External mirrors can certainly make keeping track of the road behind you a bit easier. But do you really need those large mirrors shown in Fig. 11-3? If you have a set, drive with your window open and listen to the roar. Move your hand through the area behind the mirror and feel the turbulence.

Turbulence is money going down a rat hole. Outside mirrors should be kept at the minimum size necessary to furnish the information required for safe driving. Buying a set that fair smoothly into the body is better. If you can't find a faired set to fit your car, make a set of fairings. Use plastic foam such as Styrofoam to form the outlines and cover it with a light layer of fiberglass and resin. Sand it smooth and finish with matching paint. You can find specific instructions for handling fiberglass at the library. The process of making your own mirror fairings is not at all difficult. You can use the same process to make other fairings.

A few years ago the fad in some parts of the country was to hang a squirrel tail from the end of the radio antenna. I never knew why, but few fads have any logical origin. Squirrel tails have nearly disappeared from antennas, but they have been replaced by flags and pennants and colored plastic balls. I agree that having some sort of visual identifier on your car can be helpful in large parking

Fig. 11-3. The owner of this pickup is really into seeing what is behind him. That's good, but the result is lots of noise and more drag than he realizes. A little planning could consolidate the two mirrors. Perhaps a better planning system could be designed.

lots, but they add little to the aesthetics of your car. You can argue that they take little from the performance, but when you are looking for top performance every little bit counts. Airplane designers looking for ultimate performance discovered that even a small antenna takes its toll in speed and increased fuel consumption. Having an array of antennas, with or without flags and pennants on your car, exacts its bit at the gasoline station.

Windshield sun visors, as shown in Fig. 11-4, create considerable fuel-robbing drag. I agree they sometimes look great. The appearance of vans seems to be particularly improved by the addition of a visor. If I had a classic car from the 40s or 50s, I would probably add a visor because visors were an authentic part of that era. But visors do add drag, lots of it. They sit in an area of high air pressure just as the air is trying desperately to make the turn over the roof and they trap that air. Try to picture what the air currents must look like as they are pushed into the area under the visor, forced forward against the movement of the vehicle, then rush over the top in a boil against the onrushing air. That's the epitome of turbulence.

Canoes and sailboards are items frequently found on top of cars in the summer. Cartop racks make transporting small boats convenient and less expensive than a trailer. If the boat or canoe is going to be used every weekend, there is a great temptation to leave the rack in place all week. I even knew one canoe owner who carried his canoe all of one summer without ever putting it in the water. Be honest with yourself about the number of times the boat will be carried and used. Empty car top racks create a lot of turbulence and drag. Just listen to them some time. If your daily commute is several miles, removing the rack when it's not in use makes sense. If you are inventive, you might want to try your hand at designing and building a car top rack that reduces drag to a very

Fig. 11-4. This sun visor looks great but it probably costs about one mile per gallon in gas mileage. It likely makes a lot of noise, too.

small amount. You could use some of the same techniques suggested for building fairings above.

Listen to your car as you drive. Feel it. If you hear noise or feel vibrations, you are hearing the sound of money slipping away from you. You might want to make a hobby of getting the outside lines of your car as smooth as possible. Such a hobby is better than collecting pet rocks.

12
CHAPTER

Engine, Gears, and Tire Size

THE BIG TOPIC OF CONVERSATION WHEN PERFORMANCE CAR OWNERS GET together is engine size and horsepower. Engine size is easy to determine. Just consult the manual if the engine has not been bored and stroked. If the cylinders have been bored and/or the crankshaft has been stroked, just make a couple of measurements and do a bit of math and you have the answer. Horsepower is more elusive and, therefore, more subject to the magic of imagination. The car owner who can honestly state the horsepower of his engine hasn't been born. Even if he pulled off of the dynamometer 15 minutes ago and has the ticket in his hand, he still can't give the honest figures. He will be unalterably convinced that the dyno wasn't accurate.

Does engine size really make a difference? Is the horsepower that important? You'd better believe it. Why else do we spend so much money extracting the last possible bit of power? But what is horsepower, anyway? Is it just another one of those magic numbers? How about torque? What is it and what does it do? Which is more important, horsepower or torque?

HORSEPOWER, TORQUE, AND PERFORMANCE

Horsepower and torque are related but vastly different. Torque is the measure of twisting force. That's all, just force. Horsepower is related to force, time, and distance. Torque is not related to either time or distance. Torque is the force that twists the driveshaft and turns the wheels. Horsepower gives the top speed. Peak horsepower is fun to talk about and it keeps you moving down the road once you've reached high speed. Torque is the force that boots you in the rear, climbs the mountain, and gets you off the line. You can have torque without horsepower, but you can't have horsepower without torque.

Torque is easy to measure. Figure 12-1 shows a downward force of 200 lbs. being exerted on the end of a lever two feet long. Torque is the force multiplied by the length of the lever and expressed as pounds feet. In common usage torque is expressed as foot pounds. In the example, the torque is 400 foot pounds. Where did the downward force come from? It could be any force, but assume that I weigh 200 lbs. and I'm sitting on the end of the lever. Is whatever the lever is attached to moving? No, I'm just sitting there and the lever is not moving, but the downward force exists and is called torque.

In an engine, torque is the twisting force applied to the crankshaft by the pressure on the pistons. The fuel mixture burns in the cylinders and exerts pressure against the pistons. The amount of the force depends on many factors. Some of them are the displacement or size of the engine, the compression ratio, the amount of fuel mixture in the cylinder(s), the burning characteristics of the fuel, the length of the crankshaft throw or stroke. There are others, but these are the ones we can most easily discuss. In general, the larger the engine displacement and the longer the stroke, the greater the torque.

Horsepower is torque exerted through time and distance. Because time and distance can be expressed as speed, horsepower might be stated as the speed at which torque is exerted. A small amount of torque exerted at very high speed can produce high horsepower. An example is the engine in an Indy racer. Another example is the engine in your own car. Most stock engines develop peak torque at about 2,400 rpm. Because of the problems associated with getting cylinders filled with fuel mixture as speed increases, torque falls off rapidly after reaching its peak. For example, the 5 liter Chevy develops peak torque of 255 ft. lbs. at 2,400 rpm. At that speed the engine develops about 115 horsepower. As engine speed increases, horsepower climbs to a peak of 170 at 4,000 rpm. Meanwhile, torque has dropped to 220 ft. lbs. and continues to drop rapidly as engine speed increases.

Many engine builders seek very high peak horsepower. Peak horsepower requires higher and higher engine speeds. But the very factors that produce higher engine speeds and horsepower move the point of peak torque higher. As the point of peak torque moves to a higher speed, the low-speed torque is robbed. Some high-speed racing engines develop so little low-speed torque that it is necessary to push-start the cars to get them rolling. That's not the situation you want.

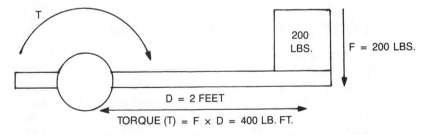

Fig. 12-1. This illustration shows that torque is just a twisting force. Torque is developed whether the shaft turns or not.

FUEL-EFFICIENT ENGINE SPEED

Another factor to consider is that most engines are most fuel-efficient when running at just slightly above peak torque speed. That is, they use fewer pounds of fuel for each horsepower developed at a speed slightly above peak torque speed. If economy is a factor, it makes sense to select or build an engine that develops peak torque at your normal engine speed.

Engine longevity is also a factor. As engine speeds increase, piston speed and wear increase rapidly. That's especially true for the long stroke engines that produce good low-speed torque.

A third factor to consider is that engines running at moderate speeds are more flexible. An engine that develops peak torque at 2,400 rpm requires less gear shifting and runs much more smoothly over the range of speeds normally used than does a higher speed engine. An extreme example is the large straight eight engines used in the 30s and 40s. It was normal to get smooth acceleration in top gear from as low as 10 mph to top speed. Those engines had peak torque speeds of as low as 2,000 rpm.

What this somewhat rambling discourse means in terms of a good engine for a street car is that such an engine should be designed to develop gobs of torque peaking at about 2,400 rpm. If the engine can be designed so that the peak of the torque curve is fairly flat, so much the better. Careful attention to such things as intake manifold design, carburetor size, camshaft timing, and exhaust tubing size will flatten the peak torque curve. Engine size, particularly length of stroke, will give you the torque you need.

APPROPRIATE ENGINE SIZE

How much torque do you need? Most enthusiasts would say that there is never enough. I write for a number of RV magazines. Engine size is very important for RV owners. My first law of engine is: ''The amount of power you don't buy is exactly equal to the amount of power needed to get you over the next mountain.'' Of course, there are limits to that philosophy. A monster Ford 460 would be somewhat out of place in a Pinto. (But it sure would be fun.)

We all want a little more engine than we have even if we can't demonstrate a real need. Perhaps the wanting is sufficient need. One of the reasons we are car enthusiasts is that we like the feeling of power at our control. I won't argue with that.

One drawback to engines with gobs of power is that they do have to be fed. For the same amount of horsepower developed, a large engine will likely require a bit more fuel than a small engine. As a balance to that bit of misfortune, the large engine will develop more torque at a usable speed and be easier to drive. Take your choice.

POWER DEPENDS ON ENGINE SIZE

There is a way to have most of the advantages of both worlds. A truism in building high torque engines is that you can't beat displacement. But there is a way that you can trick an engine into believing and performing as if it were larger than it is. The reason large engines develop more power than small engines at the same rpm is that they burn larger amounts of fuel mixture. That seems obvious, but it needs a bit more explanation.

Pressure is developed when air is burned. (To simplify things, from here on I'll refer to the fuel/air mixture as air. We both understand that air won't burn without fuel mixed in.) Larger engines are capable of burning more air than smaller engines. When the piston moves down on the intake stroke, outside air pressure tries to fill the cylinder. Because of all the restrictions of air cleaner, carburetor, intake manifold, and valve chamber design, the cylinder never is completely filled, but let's assume that it is. Let's assume a 300-cubic-inch engine. With each two revolutions that engine has the capability of burning no more than 300 cubic inches of air. At part throttle it will be burning a lot less. When you come to a hill or want to pass another car, you floor the gas pedal and the engine starts burning 300 cubic inches of air. That's all. But suppose there was a way to make that engine believe it had 450 inches of displacement. Suppose there was a way to get it to burn 450 cubic inches of air. It would have the internal friction of a 300-inch engine but would develop the power of a 450-inch engine. Rather than carry around the weight and friction of the 450-inch engine you have a light weight, low friction 300 incher. Can it be done? Yes.

As a normally aspirated engine, our 300 incher depends on atmospheric pressure to fill the cylinders. As I've already said, even at wide open throttle, the cylinders are never completely filled. But suppose that instead of depending on atmospheric pressure there was a high capacity pump to fill the cylinders. Suppose that the pump was capable of a pressure of seven pounds above atmospheric pressure. Then not only could the engine be filled, but the air could be somewhat compressed. The result would be that the engine could burn not less than 300 cubic inches but perhaps as much as 450 cubic inches. The engine would perform as if it had a displacement of 450 cubic inches. It would be like having an extra engine of 150 cubic inches waiting over in the corner to add its power whenever it was needed. Can this miracle be true? Yep.

SUPERCHARGING FOR POWER

There are such pumps. They are called superchargers or blowers. Superchargers are mounted in the intake system and, when needed, blow the charge of air into the cylinder at a pressure of up to seven pounds or so. At part throttle, for example when cruising, the pump just sits there. It runs but it doesn't pressurize. Then when additional power is needed and the throttle is opened, the supercharger begins to blow in additional air up to the pressure that it has been set for.

There are two types of superchargers categorized by the way they are powered. The older type, powered directly by belt from the engine, is still called a supercharger. The more recently developed type is powered by the expanding exhaust gases from the engine and is called a turbocharger. Both types have been in use in various types of industrial and aircraft engines for decades. The supercharger has been the darling of dragsters and others after brute horsepower for many years, but was never popular on passenger cars until recently. Turbochargers have become commonplace on diesel engines and have within the past few years become popular on sporty cars.

There are significant differences between the two. Superchargers, illustrated in Fig. 12-2, take power from the engine. The amount depends on how much pressure they are making, but can run as high as 15 horsepower at full throttle. The moving parts of the supercharger consist of a set of gears and a rotor operating at engine speed or up to twice engine speed. Since the rotor does not depend on high speed and is always running at operating speed, its response is instantaneous. You press the accelerator and the boost pressure is there instantaneously. There is no lag.

Turbochargers are powered by exhaust gases passing through a small turbine. The turbine is on one end of a shaft with the impeller on the other end. Since the impeller operates as a centrifugal blower, it needs to run at very high speed, up to 100,000 rpm. At part throttle the turbine and impeller are moving at relatively low speed. When the throttle is opened there is a discernible lag

Fig. 12-2. A supercharger can be used to make a small engine perform like one much larger. (Photo courtesy of Weiand Automotive.)

while the turbocharger comes up to speed before any boost is available. Theoretically, the turbocharger is run on waste power from the engine and costs nothing to operate.

Both types of blowers have been well proven in service. Both accomplish the task they were designed for, increasing the power of an engine over what it could normally produce. Each has advantages and disadvantages. Each can be retrofitted to most popular engines.

As with all good things, there are some caveats. Because additional power is being produced, there is additional heat to be disposed of. A larger radiator should be installed and additional heat shielding may be needed for the passenger compartment. Also, because additional air is being pushed into the cylinders, detonation can become a problem. Supercharged engines of either type should probably have a compression ratio no greater than about 8:1. That's not to say that higher compression ratios can't be used. They can be and are, but extra care is needed to avoid ping and detonation.

There are four ways of handling the problem of ping. One is to use high octane fuel. That is only a partial solution because there is no really high octane fuel available. Some owners install a water injection system that operates only when boost is being produced. The injection of small amounts of water into the intake system cools the mixture and slows down combustion. Many owners are installing an intercooler. When the air is compressed by the supercharger the temperature of the air goes up. A hot air/fuel mixture burns more rapidly than a cool mixture and is more likely to cause ping. An intercooler placed between the blower and the engine cools the air somewhat, allowing greater boost pressures and to some degree alleviating the problem of ping. Other owners and some OEM installations are using an electronic device that automatically retards the spark whenever the first sign of ping occurs. The device was discussed in chapter 7 with ignition systems.

None of the systems are 100 percent foolproof. The automatic spark retard comes closest. The combination of an intercooler and spark retard would likely handle any reasonable requirements.

GEARING AND TIRE SIZE

Earlier I mentioned that most engines are most fuel efficient when running at slightly above peak torque speed. That is the speed at which the least amount of fuel per horsepower developed is used. In the case of the 5 liter Chevy engine, the most fuel-efficient speed would be about 2,400 rpm. At that speed the engine is capable of developing 115 horsepower at wide open throttle. It can also develop only 30 horsepower at that engine speed at light throttle. As an example, suppose you're sitting in your driveway with the engine turning 2,400 rpm. Obviously, it must be developing some power. It's running and overcoming its internal friction, it's powering the fan and alternator, and you may have the air conditioner running. Call it 30 horsepower. But the car is not moving. The point is that the engine is capable of developing up to 115 horsepower at that engine speed, but it can also develop less than that. Moving your car at a steady highway speed of 55 mph in still air may require as little as 50 horse-power. That engine can develop 50 horsepower at any engine speed from 1,200 rpm on up to its red line. Why not gear for 1,200 rpm at 55 mph, then? Simply because the engine requires more pounds of fuel per horsepower at 1,200 rpm than at 2,400 rpm. An additional factor is that when turning at 2,400 rpm the engine has much more reserve power capability. So let's gear for 2,400 rpm at 55 mph.

How do you do that? By selecting the right size tires and gears. Tires are an important part of gearing. It is important to know the size tires before you can select the right gears. One popular size tire on light trucks, for example, turns 682 times to go one mile. Another popular size tire on the same size trucks turns 753 times to go the same mile. Does it make a difference? Believe it. Using the same gears with each size tire can make a difference of 230 rpm in engine speed. Doesn't sound like much, does it; but it's enough to put one of the engines well below its best economy and best pulling speed. Tire sizes do make a difference.

To determine the correct gears for your car, first select your tires. You need tires that will carry your load and give the handling performance you want. The subject was covered in depth in chapter 5. Carefully measure the diameter of the tire when mounted on the wheel and supporting the weight of the car. You don't have them yet? Then find a car that has tires the size you're going to get and measure them. Measure from the pavement to the top of the tire. Determine the engine speed you're after, peak torque speed or slightly higher. Then use the following equation. Axle ratio = (rpm × tire diameter)/(mph × 336). The result will not likely come out exactly the same as stock ratios available. Pick the closest one. If you want to see what engine speed you're getting with your present setup use the following equation. RPM = (mph × gear ratio × 336)/tire diameter. Don't know your gear ratio? Jack up one rear wheel and block the others so the car won't move. Rotate the rear wheel until the driveshaft is located so that one of the universal joint yokes is pointed right at you. Slowly rotate the tire two complete turns while you count the turns of the driveshaft. That's the gear ratio. Assume the driveshaft turned 3½ turns. The gear ratio is 3.50:1.

OVERDRIVES AND UNDERDRIVES

There are car and truck owners with special situations that no one set of gears can satisfy. There are also some who just like to play around with something a bit different.

Some owners like to have a vehicle that has excellent performance and handling on the street for the majority of their driving, but who find it convenient to use the same vehicle part of the time for heavy-duty use. Pulling a camping or travel trailer would be an example. Obviously, hanging an extra 5,000 lbs. on the back of a vehicle is going to make a difference in the way it performs. The same set of gears that are perfect for cruising a 4,000 lb. light truck are going to be somewhat less than perfect for moving a gross of 9,000 lbs. (You have to include the weight of fuel, passengers, food, and clothing.) Some sort of compromise has to be made. An overdrive or underdrive might be the answer.

First, what are these drives? I like to look at them as auxiliary transmissions because that's what they are. The names over- and underdrive can be misleading. Many stock transmissions include a top gear that is called an overdrive. To understand why, let's take a look at part of the transmission. All transmissions contain various internal gear ratios. All they do is take the input speed of the engine crankshaft and, through sets of gears, change that speed to some output speed which is fed to the driveshaft. Traditionally, the top gear in a transmission furnished an output speed equal to the input speed. Top gear was said to have a ratio of 1:1. Then someone decided there were some advantages to furnishing a gear above that for easy cruising. Since this meant that the output speed of the transmission would be greater than the input speed, this new top gear was called an overdrive. The usual overdrive ratio is about .70:1. This, too, is confusing because the output speed with an overdrive of .70:1 is actually 1.3 times the input speed. Got it? Hang on to it.

Built-in overdrives of this type are simply one additional gear. The aftermarket auxiliary transmissions fit either behind or in front of the stock transmission and permit two ratios, each of which can be used with all of the gears in the transmission. One of the ratios will be 1:1 and the other will be about .70:1. These auxiliary transmissions give six forward speeds from a stock three-speed transmission. Some of the auxiliaries, those called overdrives, have an output speed greater than the input speed. Underdrives have an output speed less than the input speed.

How can you use one? Suppose you are an owner of a light truck that sometimes pulls a 4,000 lb. travel trailer. If you are stuck with having only one set of gears, which do you gear for, the solo truck or the truck and trailer? With an auxiliary transmission you can gear for both. I have such a situation. I selected an engine and rear end gear ratio that would be suited for pulling the trailer. That left me with more power than necessary when not pulling the trailer. I added an auxiliary gear box with an overdrive output. Now I can pull the trailer easily and still have low engine speeds when running solo. I realize that the rear end gears put my engine at its most fuel-efficient speed and would be suitable for running solo. But I also realize that I don't like the additional wear on the engine running at that speed when it's not necessary. In my case, I have a huge engine that loafs along in overdrive. The saving in engine speed and noise is worth it. Besides, I'm a bit of a nut.

If I had started with a vehicle with higher gears (lower numerical) for solo cruising or an engine that was a bit smaller than ideal for pulling, I could have used an auxiliary with an output speed lower than input speed and accomplished roughly the same thing. By using the auxiliary transmission with each of the automatic's gears, I have six forward speeds with speeds between those in the automatic. When climbing mountains with the trailer, I have a gear that lets the engine run at its most efficient speed regardless of road speed, just like the 18-wheelers.

There are different types of auxiliary transmissions for different applications. Doug Nash Engineering and Gear Vendors both build auxiliaries that replace the tailshaft of the popular large Ford and GM automatics. Both make simple installations. The Doug Nash unit uses straight-cut gears and can run continually in either ratio. The Gear Vendors box uses planetary gears, can be used in overdrive only in forward gear on the automatic, and will engage in overdrive only at speeds over 20 mph. Mitchell and Advance Adaptors have auxiliaries for use with manual transmissions. Addresses are given in the Appendix.

13
CHAPTER

Oil Smooths the Way

OIL IS SLIPPERY STUFF. IT ALSO HAS A CLINGING QUALITY THAT MAKES IT HANG onto anything it touches. And, ask the mother of any teenager who likes to hang around cars—oil is dirty. Engine oil operates in one of the most hostile environments imaginable, the engine room of a car or truck. Combustion chamber temperatures may well run from 2,000 to 3,000 degrees. Valve heads reach temperatures of 2,000 degrees. Piston heads frequently operate at over 1,000 degrees. It's a hot, dirty job but somebody has to do it. Fortunately, oil does it well.

OIL DOES MORE THAN LUBRICATE

One of oil's most important tasks is to make engine parts slippery and keep moving parts separate from each other. The film of oil separating the important bearing parts of crankshaft journals and connecting rod bearings might be only .0001 inch thick. The pressure is so great you don't even want to hear about it. Let that film of oil break down for even a minute and your engine is history. The entire life and safety of your multithousand-dollar engine rests on the protection of a $1.00 quart of oil. Think about it. A tiny genuflect in the direction of Pennsylvania would not be amiss.

But there's more. We think of our engines as being water-cooled, but those five quarts of oil in the crankcase soak up as much as 20 percent of the engine's heat. Oil plays an important part in cooling the engine. It gets to the really hot spots that water can't reach and carries the heat away. In the process, the oil might reach temperatures of 300 degrees.

Modern oils contain a detergent to help keep the internal parts of the engine clean. The processes of combustion result in all sorts of nasty by-products. Most of them are blown out the exhaust system, but some find their way into the engine's vital organs. If allowed to remain there, they combine to form acids that don't do the metal parts any good. Some of the by-products form solids that can become abrasive if allowed to remain in contact with wear areas. It is the job of the engine oil to remove these by-products and carry them to the oil filter.

Whenever a gallon of gasoline is burned, a gallon of water is produced. Think of it: every 25 miles your engine produces a gallon of water. Most of the water is blown out the exhaust pipe, but some finds its way past the piston rings into the crankcase. If allowed to remain there, the water combines with other products of combustion to form acids and sludge. Sludge blocks tiny oil passages and generally gums up the works. We know what acid does. Oil has to protect against the damage.

Oil also serves as a seal between piston rings and cylinder walls. If it were not for this sealing action, a portion of the burning gases of combustion would force their way past the pistons instead of supplying power to the pistons. All that stops those hot gases is a tiny film of oil .0001 inch thick trying to do its job while the temperatures shoot up to 3,000 degrees and the piston rings keep moving. An impossible task.

Finally, you spent a lot of money for that engine. Most of it is made of some compound of iron. When iron comes in contact with the moisture in the air, or the products of combustion, it rusts. Water vapor is the natural enemy of iron. Not only does rust remove tiny amounts from the metal, but those rust particles can become erosive materials if permitted to remain. One of oil's tasks is to prevent rust and corrosion within the engine.

All that for a buck a can. It makes oil sound like the bargain of the century. It is. Without some sort of lubricant, we simply would not have the machines of transportation and industry. Our cars and factories could not exist.

CHOOSING THE RIGHT OIL

Not so long ago in a land not so far away, the choices were easy. Engines were much simpler and operating conditions were less stringent. Expectations were far less, too. I clearly remember that when I bought my first car, a used Chevy, the salesman told me that burning a quart of oil for each five gallons of gasoline was not excessive. Can you imagine? Given the mileage attainments of the day, that was a quart every 75 miles. In addition, we took it for granted that oil changes were done every 1,000 miles. A valve job was anticipated every 25,000 miles and a complete overhaul every 50,000 to 60,000 miles. No driver would accept those conditions today. As a contrast, the van I'm driving has over 135,000 miles on the engine, the heads have never been removed, and I get about 2,000 miles to the quart of oil. Some difference.

What has brought these differences? Well, engines are made differently. Tolerances are much closer, better metals are used, parts are given a superior finish, and filtration of intake air and oil are much improved. Along with these improvements have come higher power outputs. The same size engine that once produced 75 horsepower now produces 200 horsepower. That additional power puts additional stress on all engine parts. Oil has a bigger job to do.

When I bought the first Chevy, the oil choices were brand and viscosity. All oils were straight mineral oils with no additives. Because I lived in the North, I used straight 10 in the winter and 40 in the summer. Woe unto the driver who delayed changing from 40 to 10. I once saw a car with summer weight oil being pushed by a service truck in subzero weather. The truck roared, the car's tires squealed, but the engine didn't turn over.

Now things are different. As engines became more sophisticated, operating temperatures increased, combustion by-products proliferated, and the demands on oil zoomed. Now oils are graded by service application. Engine manufacturers continually require better protection from engine oil. As Fig. 13-1 shows, the oil can has markings to show what kind of service it is intended for. The SF marking indicates that the oil meets the latest manufacturers' requirements for gasoline engines. By the time this book is on the shelf, that service requirement will likely have been changed to SG. The CC marking indicates that the oil is approved for use in diesel engines with C service requirements.

The SAE marking gives the viscosity, or flow, rating. The Society of Automotive Engineers has established various flow rates at high and low temperatures and assigned them numbers. The lower the number, the easier the oil will flow. Subzero temperatures impose difficult flow conditions on oil. The W following the SAE number indicates that the oil has met the flow rates of these winter temperatures. Years ago, there was only one SAE number on a can of oil. It was marked 10W for winter use or 40 for summer use. That didn't work too badly when oil was changed every 1,000 miles. Now most manufacturers

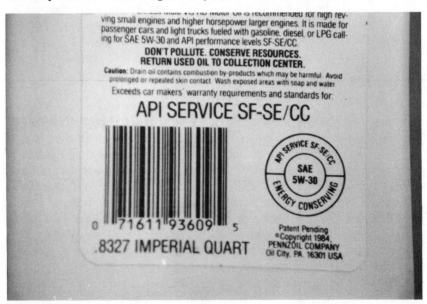

Fig. 13-1. The information on an oil container tells you a lot about its intended use. Make certain the oil you buy is correct for your engine.

suggest changing oil every 5,000 to 7,500 miles. For some drivers that can well overlap the seasonal changes. One response is the multigrade oil. SAE 10W-40 oil is supposed to flow like 10W oil in very cold temperatures and maintain its film strength like 40 oil in high temperatures. Nearly all manufacturers today recommend the use of multigrade oil.

The last few years have brought an additional marking. Some oils make the claim to be Energy Conserving. Before being permitted to place this marking on the can, the oil manufacturer must show that an engine using the oil has achieved a slightly greater fuel economy than the same engine with another oil used as a base. The difference is slight, something just over 1 percent.

Diesel engines produce combustion by-products different from those of gasoline engines. The operating environment is also different. The result is that diesel engines' lubricating requirements are different from those of gasoline engines. Until recently, separate oils were produced. Now most oil companies combine the requirements for both engines into one oil. If you drive a diesel, just be sure that the oil you buy has a C rating for your engine.

CHOOSING THE RIGHT VISCOSITY

What grade of oil should you use? First, let's deal with quality. There was a time when there were vast differences between brands of oils. The forces of competition have removed most of those differences. Consumer's Union, an independent consumer testing agency, says that all brands are not created equal. Their tests show that some brands of oil are clearly superior to other brands in some areas. Since the picture is changing from time to time, I suggest you check their report, which is published periodically. Your public library will have the information.

There are numerous mechanics and owners who claim that there is no problem with mixing brands of oil. I disagree. If there are differences among the brands, then mixing brands can only result in some degradation of quality. I insist on using the same brand in my engine at all times. To be sure that I can do this if a quart is needed on a trip, I always carry a few quarts in a box. The only time I would mix brands would be in an emergency. Any oil is better than no oil.

As to viscosity, your manufacturer has suggestions for you based on expected temperature extremes and anticipated driving conditions. I suggest you follow those recommendations when you can. Some recent recommendations do bother me a bit. Most manufacturers recommend 5W-30 oil for nearly year-round use with the following caveat: Do not use 5W-30 for sustained high-speed driving. With current speed limits being 55 or 65 mph, what constitutes high-speed driving? What do they mean by sustained? If I hit the expressway for a two hour trip at 65, am I risking my engine with 5W-30? Does the manufacturer seriously believe that I can take the time to change the oil to make a trip across the state, then change it back for the next week's "normal" driving? Perplexing.

I've solved the problem on my wife's car—my van would die of apoplexy if I poured a can of 5W-anything in it—by using 5W-30 in the winter regardless of trips and 10W-30 in the summer. It seems to work.

There are still many unregenerated throwbacks to the 40s who believe that straight grades of oil are the best. They use straight 30 or 40 or 10 according to the prevailing temperatures. If their engine is never going to see temperatures of less than 80 degrees, they might be right in using 40. I can't guarantee those operating conditions. I also worry about those few minutes when the engine is first started. Those are the hardest minutes on any engine. The oil has drained out of many operating parts. There are several long moments before oil pressure pumps fresh oil to the bearings. The heavier the oil, the longer it takes to reach the bearings. I don't like it. I use multigrade oil.

SYNTHETIC OR PETROLEUM-BASED OIL

Here's another decision we've only recently had to make. New jet and turboprop aircraft engines imposed lubricating conditions that petroleum-based oils found it difficult to meet. The chemical industry responded by compounding synthetic bases for lubricants. Ethylene gas is the main building block of synthetic oil. Ethylene gas is obtained by various chemical actions from coal, natural gas, or crude oil. In the laboratory, ethylene is combined with various other products to form the base oil stock. Then it is combined with special additives to produce the specific qualities required. The result can be a superior product with extreme consistency.

How does synthetic oil compare with petroleum-based oil? In basic operating terms, an engine is hard to start when it is cold. Petroleum oil, even 5W, offers more resistance than synthetic oil. In very cold weather an engine with synthetic oil is easier to start.

Petroleum oil is sensitive to temperature. It begins to oxidize and break down when temperatures exceed 220 degrees. Oil producers add various compounds to counteract or delay the breakdown, but they are only partially successful. Synthetic oils are stable at temperatures above 400 degrees with some manufacturers claiming safe operation at 600 degrees.

Petroleum oil thins out as it heats up. To control this effect, refiners add viscosity improvers. The viscosity improvers are supposed to permit the oil to be thin in cold temperatures but cause it to become thicker as the temperatures rise. Unfortunately, the viscosity improvers are the first victims of temperatures above 220 degrees. Synthetic oils are not affected by high temperatures, maintaining their viscosity regardless of the temperature. Petroleum oils start thin and get thinner as the temperature rises. Synthetic oils start out even thinner but don't change in response to temperature increases.

Petroleum oil is an excellent lubricant. But its lubricating qualities change as a result of time and use. Synthetic oils are much more stable and retain their lubricating qualities longer.

Synthetic oil might cost up to six times as much as petroleum oil. Is it worth the additional cost? Proving that wear characteristics of synthetic oil are better is difficult. Few owners have the time, money, or facilities to tear down an engine after 50,000 miles and measure the wear and then repeat the test with an identical engine with the other oil. If the oil companies are performing such tests, they aren't talking about the results. If you've been getting 100,000 miles of trouble-free wear with petroleum oil, getting you interested in even better wear with synthetic oil may be a bit difficult.

Auto company personnel are adamant in their opposition to an extended drain period with synthetic oil. Petroleum engineers are aghast at the idea of running any oil for 15,000 miles. Synthetic oil engineers maintain that 15,000 mile drain intervals are not only practical, but often suggest 25,000 mile drain periods.

OIL DRAIN INTERVAL

Drain interval is a hot topic for discussion. With petroleum oils, the oils break down over a period of time. Combustion by-products find their way into the crankcase and the oil. Wear particles also pollute the oil. The conventional wisdom is that the oil must be drained frequently to remove all these contaminants and supply fresh lubricant. The synthetic oil engineers claim that petroleum oil itself is part of the problem, that much of the contamination is caused by the presence of the oil. I have seen reports that verified that.

It is common practice to drain oil from an engine, add fresh oil, and have the fresh oil looking as black as the old oil within only a few minutes of running. This discoloration comes from the sludge and other contamination that never really get removed from the engine. I have had only one engine in which I used synthetic oil. At the first oil change I switched to synthetic. I maintained a drain period of 15,000 miles with a filter change at about 8,000 miles. When I sold the car at 30,000 miles the oil was still nearly as clean and clear as when it was added.

My personal beliefs are that if you start with a newly broken-in engine with tight seals, synthetic oil is superior to petroleum oil. I would suggest changing it at 20,000 miles and changing the filter at 8,000 and 15,000 miles on each oil change. If driving conditions are severely dusty, an early change would be prudent.

For those who use petroleum oil, the question of drain periods is a bit different. Typically, a car manufacturer will advertise that his car requires an oil change only every 7,500 miles. Long drain periods sell cars. The less frequently a car needs service the less service will cost. Manufacturers are fond of pointing to every possibility that their cars are cheaper to operate. But, if you look at the fine print, you might find something else. The 7,500-mile drain period applies unless you operate under severe conditions. As the car manufacturers define it, severe service means most trips are less than four miles, or most trips are less than 10 miles and outside temperatures remain below freezing, or the engine is permitted to idle for extended periods of time, or you tow a trailer, or you drive in dusty areas. Thought you were normal, didn't you? If you meet any of the above conditions, you're not—at least your driving is not. Under those conditions you should change your oil and filter every 3,000 miles.

So what do you do? My mechanic friends say to change your oil every 2,000 miles regardless of the kind of driving. Most of them suggest a filter change every second or third change. That makes sense. Next to your home, your car is the most expensive thing you buy. Its value is expected to begin decreasing immediately and reach zero at some time in the future. Along the way, it is expected to require some amount of expensive repair. The longer it takes your car to reach zero value, and the less the cost of the repairs along the way, the better. Good maintenance tips the odds in your favor. Ten bucks for an oil change every 2,000 miles strikes me as being pretty cheap insurance for an expensive product.

OIL ADDITIVES

Every oil manufacturer believes in the necessity of additives to his oil. The only problem: he insists that those additives be only the ones he puts in. Oil is full of additives. Pour-point depressants are added to keep the oil from congealing into a chunk of wax when it gets cold. Oxidation inhibitors are added to slow down the rate of oxidation. Without it oil mixes with oxygen and loses its lubrication qualities. Corrosion inhibitors are added to control the corrosion to bearings and other engine parts when the engine is not running. Detergents are added to help keep the engine clean and keep combustion by-products in suspension. (It always bothers me a bit that the oil is designed to keep that crud in suspension and circulating back through the engine. I guess at least some of it is supposed to stay in suspension until it reaches the filter.)

Foam inhibitors are needed to break down the air bubbles that form as the oil is squirted here and there and splashed around the innards of the engine. I've already mentioned viscosity improvers to counteract the oil's normal tendencies to change viscosity. Extreme pressure additives are needed to protect various parts of the engine that operate under extremely high pressures and temperatures. Friction modifiers are added to some oils to make them slicker and deliver a tiny bit more mileage. Did I leave anything out? Is there any room left for oil?

Clearly all of these additives are needed or the manufacturers wouldn't go to the expense of putting them in. Some are required to meet engine manufacturers' requirements for their new engines. Do you need to add more? If you go through the auto department of any variety store or visit a parts shop, you'll find plenty more additives. Read the advertising claims and you'll come away confused. They all claim that, in spite of the long list of additives already in the oil, more is needed.

Frankly, I doubt it. There is some evidence that adding more chemicals can cause trouble. The notion is that indiscriminate mixing of compounds can upset the balance and lessen their effectiveness. I don't know about that, but I'm reasonably sure that top quality oils today offer about all that can be offered. Unless you have a special problem and know what you're doing, save your money for something else.

TIME TO CHANGE OIL

Even with synthetic oil, there eventually comes a time to get rid of the old and put in the new. Even with the best of care and best oil, there are contaminants that find their way to the crankcase. The older and more worn the engine, the easier it is for the contaminants to gain entry. Left in the oil they increase wear and corrosion. Get them out.

City driving is probably the hardest type of driving for an engine. That's especially true in cold weather. Every gallon of gasoline burned produces a gallon of water. Most of the water goes out the tail pipe, but some, too much, finds its way into the crankcase. If the engine is allowed to warm up fully and is run for at least a half hour each time it is started, the excess water is removed. Normal driving in traffic in the wintertime doesn't get the engine hot enough.

Frequent draining of old oil is the easiest and cheapest way to assure that your engine remains clean and free of contaminants. Engines that don't get frequent oil changes accumulate quantities of sludge. The sludge tends to block small, internal oil passages. If the oil doesn't get through, some engine part isn't going to be lubricated and will wear out prematurely. As a classic example, several years ago I worked for a service station owner who didn't believe in changing the oil in his car, ever. He simply added oil when necessary. He proved the worth of his theory by buying a new Plymouth and running it for 50,000 miles with not one oil change. Then at 50,000 miles he changed the oil, the crankshaft, the rods and bearings, the pistons and rings, and the camshaft and bearings. As the mechanic said, "Pay me now or pay me later."

Changing your oil is an easy but dirty maintenance job you can do. The savings are appreciable. You can buy the same oil the service station uses for less at discount stores. Ditto for the oil filter. Buy a plastic drain tub with a pour spout. You'll need a 10-inch crescent wrench for the drain plug and a filter wrench for the filter. You'll also need some old rags for the mess.

Run the engine for a few minutes to get the oil warm so that it will flow more readily. Put some old papers under the engine and the drain tub on the papers. Use the crescent wrench to loosen the drain plug. It will be warm. Let the oil drain completely before replacing the drain plug. Tighten snugly with the wrench.

Slide the papers and drain tub under the filter. Things can get a little tricky here. Some of the newer toy cars are quite crowded in the engine compartment. Access to the filter might require some physical contortions, but you can manage. Use the filter wrench to loosen the filter a couple of turns. Remove the filter and let it drain into the drain tub. With your finger, smear a coating of oil on the gasket of the new filter. Install the new filter and turn it until the gasket surface touches the engine surface. Give it another ¾ turn. That should be enough.

Remove the drain tub from under the car and place it out of the way. Add the required amount of new oil. Check your owner's manual for the amount. Don't forget to add some for the filter. Start up the engine and let it run for a few minutes. Inspect the oil filter for leaks. If there are any, tighten a bit more. Overtightening can warp the filter surface and cause a leak.

Pour the old oil into empty plastic gallon jugs and dispose of properly. Most garages will accept used oil. Many villages and cities have oil disposal tanks in convenient locations. Whatever you do, don't pour the oil on the ground unless you like the notion of drinking used motor oil in your drinking water. Clean everything up and congratulate yourself. You just saved about $10 that can be better spent for gasoline.

KEEP IT CLEAN

Oil filters have the important task of removing quantities of crud from the oil. Some of the crud, surprisingly, is sand. Other parts are bits of metal that are worn from the engine. Some is dust that finds its way into the engine. Without the filter to remove this material, it will continue to circulate through the engine with the oil. Each passage will extract its bit in additional wear and hasten the day when major repairs are due.

Different filter manufacturers use differing kinds of filter designs and filter media. Figure 13-2 shows a cutaway of a typical oil filter. There is even one company that sells a filter that uses a roll of toilet paper as the filtering element. Most use rather sophisticated materials and designs to remove as much of the harmful material as possible. Not all the circulating grit is removed nor is it intended to be. Grit is measured in microns. A micron is one-millionth of a meter. The common grit found in crankcases ranges from 10 microns to over 50 microns in diameter. There are questions about just how much of the grit needs

Fig. 13-2. Oil filters have the important task of removing a variety of contaminants from your lubricating oil. This cutaway shows how one company's filter does it. (Photo courtesy of Allied Aftermarket Division.)

126

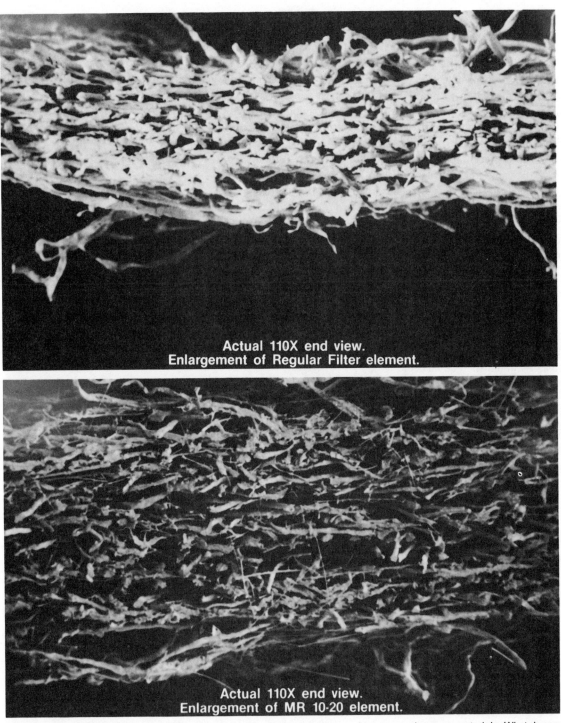

Actual 110X end view.
Enlargement of Regular Filter element.

Actual 110X end view.
Enlargement of MR 10-20 element.

Fig. 13-3. Not all filters use the same filtering media. These two are supposed to remove the same materials. What do you think? Buy a quality filter. (Photo courtesy of Allied Aftermarket Division.)

to be removed. You might say, "Hell, get it all out." The problem is that making the filtering material fine enough to remove all the grit also restricts the flow of oil. If the oil doesn't move through the filter media, it can't remove anything.

Grit that is fine enough to move between bearing surfaces isn't likely to do any damage. It might as well be left alone. Only the grit that is large enough to become lodged in those bearing surfaces can do damage. Since most of the sensitive gaps are about 38 microns, the most damaging grit would be those particles between about 20 microns and 40 microns in diameter. Filter media are generally designed to remove material within that size range. Figure 13-3 shows two different filter media enlarged 110 times. Although both are intended to do the same job, you can see that there are differences.

Almost all filters used today are the spin-on cartridge type. These are intended to be used for a period of time and replaced. In past eras, some filters had elements that you could clean periodically by washing in a solvent. These filters used very fine screens to remove the grit. Others used an element that was thrown away after use. For various reasons, convenience not the least of these, the spin-on cartridge type is the most common today.

Engine manufacturers generally recommend changing the filter with every oil change. I believe that is more frequent than necessary if the oil is changed every 2,000 to 3,000 miles. I believe that under most conditions a filter should be good for about 8,000 to 9,000 miles. The exceptions would be if the engine had been operated under very dusty conditions. Certainly, more frequent changes would then be advised.

14
CHAPTER

Mouse Milk
and Whistles

FROM THE DAY AFTER THE FIRST MAN PUT SOME SORT OF ENGINE ON A WAGON, someone else has been making something to make the engine run better. Wonder drugs for more power, spark plugs with mystical powers, magnets for the fuel lines—there has been no end of imagination and never will be. Car owners have constantly sought, and some ''engineer'' or ''chemist'' has been anxious to provide, the magical fluid or ten cent device that will make their Clark Kent Six leap tall mountains at a single bound—and run on water. (Yes, that has been tried. Several years ago there were ads in national magazines for pills that could be dropped into a tank of water converting it to motor fuel. Even Henry Ford is said to have fallen for a similar gimmick.)

A quick trip through one catalog found 23 gadgets, each guaranteed to give up to 20 percent mileage and power. A trip down the auto aisle in any discount store will reveal many more. Magazines for car owners are lined with advertisements for everything from 200 mpg carburetors to fluids that will restore worn-out engines to 75,000 volt ignition coils, to . . . . Do they work? Obviously. If they didn't work for the manufacturers and vendors, they wouldn't be so profitable. But do they meet their claims? That's a different story.

LIQUID ADDITIVES

The magic products seem to be divided into two groups—fluids and gadgets. We'll look at the fluids first. Years ago these fluids were given the slang name ''mouse milk'' because most of them were just about as effective as that esoteric product. Many of the fluids are of the oil detergent type. Until detergent oils hit the market about 30 years ago, no one had heard of detergents for cars. Then oil refiners hit on the excellent idea of adding compounds to their oils that would keep the sludge and gunk in suspension until it passed through the oil filter. Suddenly there were dozens of canned detergents on the market.

The idea was that if the oil companies thought detergents were important enough to be added to oil at the refinery, they must be good. So, step right up, Mr. and Mrs. Car Owner, and buy a can of super detergent that's guaranteed to keep your engine so clean that it will never wear out. One frequent result of this if-a-little-is-good-more-is-better attitude was a ruined engine. With the best of care, an engine accumulates sludge and carbon in its nooks and crannies. Over thousands of miles the accumulation can become extreme. When owners of these high mileage engines added an extra can of detergent, much of the sludge broke loose and began circulating. Too often a chunk lodged in an important oil passage and stopped the oil from circulating. There went the engine. The truth of the matter is that if you use a quality oil, your engine doesn't need any additional detergent in the oil.

OIL THICKENERS

Another group of additives is oil thickeners. The idea is to add a can with every oil change and seal up the worn areas with a thicker oil. If this were a good idea, it would make more sense to buy a higher viscosity oil in the first place. It is probably true that if your engine is badly worn, 40 weight oil will not go through it quite as fast as 20 weight oil. But 40 weight, being thicker, is going to require extra gasoline just to overcome the drag of the thicker oil. Thicker oil is no substitute for an engine overhaul, but it can postpone the inevitable for a short time. Just don't try 40 weight oil in the winter if you live where the temperature slips out of the bottom of the thermometer.

There is one other situation where an oil thickener might be worthwhile. Earlier I mentioned that 5W-30 oil is recommended for many new engines, but the manufacturers warn you not to use that oil for sustained high-speed driving. What do you do if your engine is full of 5W-30 and you suddenly are required to take a fast 500-mile trip? Get a quick oil change to a heavier grade? You could, and that might be the best thing to do. Or you could add a can of oil thickener.

Some producers of oil thickeners claim to have added an ingredient that makes their product cling to the bearing surfaces and not drain down when the engine is not running. The claims might be valid, but quality engine oils make the same claim. I doubt that more is needed.

ENGINE OVERHAUL IN A BOTTLE!

You can regularly see ads for a $1.98 product that is guaranteed to restore worn rings, pistons, and valves. Supposedly, there is some magic material held in suspension in a petroleum base that will adhere to the metal and make worn parts like new again. Or the product may come in the form of pills that look like aspirin tablets. Then why spend hundreds of dollars for an overhaul? Just add the magic $1.98 product and enjoy your brand-new engine. If you believe that, I'll talk to you about a piece of property I own up in Brooklyn. It's got a nice bridge and . . . .

UPPER CYLINDER LUBRICANTS

Upper cylinder lubricants have been popular for more than 60 years. The upper cylinder area is the most hostile environment in your engine. Temperatures routinely range from 2,000 to 3,000 degrees. The only lubrication the area gets is the little that's carried up from the lower cylinder area by the piston rings plus a bit that is sprayed on the valve stems. This is one place I think can use some help. Upper cylinder oils are usually added to the gasoline tank at fill-up time. A small amount of oil is drawn through the carburetor with the fuel and deposited on the valve stems and guides, the valve heads, and the upper cylinder walls. I've tried it and I like the results, but it is a nuisance. A better idea is an injector system from Marvel Oil Co. The tank holds two quarts of upper cylinder oil and injects it automatically into the intake manifold where it is drawn into the the upper cylinder area. The injector is designed to increase the flow when the engine is operating at high load conditions. The tank holds enough for up to 2,000 miles. I like the convenience. Marvel's Mystery Oil is available in most performance shops and many discount stores. (The name, Marvel Mystery Oil, supposedly comes from an early customer, who asked what was in the product that made it perform so well. The reply was, ''That's a mystery''; and the name stuck.)

I can't prove it, but I think upper cylinder lubrication has special merit today. Until the early 70s, nearly all gasoline contained minute amounts of lead. The lead was mainly used as an octane enhancer to produce the high octane fuel needed for the high compression engines popular at that time. (For those of you of tender age, gasoline with an octane rating of over 100 was commonly available. Ah, for the good old days.) Then the government decreed that we had to get the lead out to protect the quality of the air. Suddenly, it was found that lead had served another purpose. Small amounts of the lead adhered to the valve head surfaces and gave them important protection from the extreme heat of combustion. When the lead was removed, the incidence of burned valves increased. Hardened surfaces were added to compensate, but recent tests have shown that for engines under heavy-duty service even the hardened surfaces aren't enough. These are the engines used in vehicles moving heavy loads—such as trucks, tractors, and vehicles pulling trailers. There have been several products released to the market that claim to protect the valve surfaces. Some of them have proven worthwhile. I think adding upper cylinder oil also helps protect the valves of engines in heavy-duty service. Don't try using regular engine oil for upper cylinder lubrication. Some of the additives, particularly the detergents, leave harmful deposits when the oil is burned. Fouled plugs are one result.

Among the upper cylinder oils, I am reasonably confident of the value of two products. One is Marvel Mystery Oil, distributed widely for more than 65 years. The product can be added to the gasoline or used with the company's automatic injector. I've been using the injector for several years and find it very convenient. The other product is Lubrigas which is added to the gas at fill-up time. Both products seem to do exactly what they claim to do. There may be others that are just as effective, but I haven't had the opportunity to test them.

FRICTION REDUCERS

Probably for as long as there have been engines there have been products designed to decrease the internal friction. Various additives have been used from graphite to molybdenum to Teflon. All claim to add a coating to the metal that reduces friction, increases gasoline mileage, and increases engine life. Most require regular additions, usually to the crankcase at oil change time. One product that is different is Slick 50 and other brands containing Teflon. These claim to be one-time treatments that permanently deposit the Teflon on bearing and cylinder surfaces. I admit that it sounds like more mouse milk, but I've seen reports of fantastic results. I've owned or known personally of four engines treated with Slick 50. Two currently have in excess of 125,000 miles each. Of those, one with over 135,000 miles uses a quart of oil in 2,000 miles. The other uses no oil between 3,000-mile oil changes. Both are in vans used to pull travel trailers. Of the other two engines, I lost track of one after 75,000 miles. At that time it was using no oil between changes. The fourth engine has only 45,000 miles, and no oil is ever added between changes. That would be expected at such low mileage. I realize that four engines don't make for a scientific test, but I will continue to use the product as long as it is available.

Many cars built since the elimination of lead from gasoline have serious problems from ping. Even the so-called high octane gasolines don't always help. Octane enhancers are popular products that claim to alleviate the problem. I've had little personal experience with them and have read conflicting reports. Some owners have reported that the products helped. Others have been disappointed. If your engine has a ping problem that cannot be cured with any other treatment, try an octane enhancer.

GADGETS

Most of the gadgets are intended to increase gasoline mileage. Over the years I've seen such a variety, all with guaranteed claims, that if all were used at the same time and did what they were guaranteed to do, I would have to drain the excess gasoline from the tank regularly. Some of the gadgets defy belief. Screens that mount between the carburetor and the intake manifold. Idle adjustment screws that bleed additional air into the fuel mixture. Magnets that attach to the fuel line. Fans that mount in the carburetor throat. Heaters that attach to the fuel line. High intensity coils. Magic spark plugs. Vapor injectors. And more.

Each company has numerous testimonials from satisfied owners with glowing claims of impossible gasoline mileage. I hate to admit it, but I've tried a few.

Virtually none has worked. My engine would hardly run on the magic spark plugs. The vapor injector worked on one engine simply because the carburetor was set to run rich and the injector diluted the mixture. It would not produce the same results on today's lean-running engines. Logic would suggest that if a car manufacturer could increase the mileage of his cars 25 percent by adding a $3.50 gadget the company would enjoy a fantastic competitive edge.

Of course, there is the old myth of collusion between the oil companies and the car companies. That's exactly what it is, a myth. Supposedly, an engineer or gadgeteer developed a carburetor that would give 200 mpg. Fearing what would happen to their gasoline market, the oil companies paid the car companies not to use it. Another version has the oil companies buying the carburetor and patents and hiding it. Whatever, it's absurd.

The mythical carburetor keeps coming up. There are ads in some car magazines for the plans to build your own. Other ads offer to sell you the complete carburetor. Following the publication of one of my articles on fuel mileage several months ago, I received advertising material from one of these companies offering to let me test their carburetor. Of course, I agreed with the stipulation that the results would be published in my column. The president of the company promised to send me a carburetor within 30 days. That was over six months ago. I'm still waiting.

There are some gadgets that work. Computer ignition systems were discussed in chapter 7. The good ones work. I tested the Jacobs unit and got a 13 percent mileage increase while increasing the power. MSD has a computer ignition system that is a bit different but should produce similar results. The nearly universal acceptance of computer ignition systems by automobile companies proves their value. Nearly all new cars use a computer ignition.

Special high-voltage ignition coils abound. I recently saw an advertisement for a 75,000 volt coil. These, too, were discussed in chapter 7. Remember, high amperage is what gives better ignition. Voltage over 40,000 volts is an advertising gimmick.

Ping suppressors—also called timing controls—have an important advantage for engines that are used in both light and heavy service. These devices offer the owner the opportunity of adjusting the ignition advance to the existing conditions. Don't even think about taking mine away. I prefer the manually adjustable type because I like to know exactly what setting is being used. I will admit that for most owners the automatic type is possibly better. That is especially true if you have a supercharged engine. With too much boost and ignition advance, the engine could be destroyed from detonation. The automatic ping control gives protection against that possibility.

I like the theory of water injection but I haven't been able to get the promised results. The idea is that when an engine is operating under a heavy load the combustion pressures and temperatures rise, adding to the probability of ping. Injecting a tiny amount of water into the fuel mixture cools the mixture and slows down combustion. Ping is eliminated. Spark can be advanced beyond the normal setting. Additional power and acceleration can be realized.

The water injection process has been well tested and proven in everything from the fighter planes of World War II to the most modern racing engines. I know it works, but not for me. I suspect that I have been expecting too much from it. If you decide to get a water injection unit, buy one that is electronically controlled. The good ones monitor both engine rpm and manifold pressure and only inject water when rpm is high enough to handle the injection and manifold pressure indicates a heavy load. Don't fall for the water vapor injectors. They work exactly backwards from what is needed, injecting more water when manifold pressure is high than when it is low. Low manifold pressure indicates a high engine load. That's when water injection is needed.

Many middle to higher priced cars come with driving computers. They're fun. They tell you everything you could want to know about how your car is operating. Current and average fuel mileage is available at the touch of a button. Want to know your average speed since you left home? Press a button. What's the outside temperature? Press a button. How much fuel is left? At your present speed, how far can you go before running out of gas? Press a button. Most of them also include cruise control. Driving computers are great.

They likely won't save you any money and they won't make the engine develop more power, but they're fun. If your car doesn't have one, you can get an add-on model. Your local performance shop should have one or can order one for you. Some of the national catalog retailers also list them.

I like cruise control. I don't want a car or truck without it. Most expert drivers will claim that they can get better mileage than a cruise control will deliver. They're probably right. I think I can beat the cruise control, too, but I don't want to work that hard. The cruise control just keeps you humming along at the speed you select. I like it. The aftermarket models install easily and the ones I've had are reliable. Parts stores and catalog retailers make them easy to find. If you have a late model car, you can probably get the stock cruise control from your car dealer. It will cost a bit more than an aftermarket model, but it will look and act as if it came from the factory.

Most cruise controls have adjustments for engaging speed and sensitivity. You can save gas by not setting the sensitivity too high. Letting the car lose three or four mph while climbing hills saves gas. The sensitivity control lets you adjust the amount of speed variation allowed.

Every vehicle should have a tachometer. It's impossible to be sure of your engine speed without one. Using a tachometer is the only way you can know when to downshift to keep the engine operating at peak efficiency. Tachometers are readily available, inexpensive, and easy to install. The top engine speed covered ranges from 6,000 rpm up to 12,000 rpm. It might be fun to see 12,000 on your tachometer, but the fact is your engine will rarely turn more than 4,000 rpm. Choosing a realistic top range on your tachometer increases the ease of reading it because the scale will be more widely spaced.

Vacuum gauges are also readily available and easy to install. A vacuum gauge is useful in determining how hard your engine is pulling, but its greatest benefit is as a diagnostic tool. By keeping track of vacuum readings over a period of time you can determine when the engine needs a tune-up or repair. A vacuum gauge will indicate when your muffler is plugged. The chart that comes with your gauge will give lots of suggestions for reading engine ailments. Mechanics use a vacuum gauge with a 4-inch face. That's a little large for mounting permanently on your dash. Buy one of the smaller units that can be mounted in the dash or in a separate subpanel.

Using gadgets can be fun. I admit to being a gadget addict. I like dials and gauges. Keeping track of what's happening with my engines adds to the pleasure of driving. There are worse things to do while you're driving. Of course, I'm not suggesting that you should keep your eyes glued to the dials and try to drive on instruments. That could be hazardous to your health and to mine.

APPENDIX

Sources for Parts, Tools, and Information

THE FIRST REACTION FROM MANY OWNERS WHO NEED PARTS IS TO HEAD FOR their new car dealer. That's logical. After all, a Ford dealer should have all the parts needed for your Ford and a Chevy dealer would be expected to have Chevy parts. You would also expect to find the best parts for your car at the factory's local dealer. The fact is that many parts on your car as it came from the factory were not made by the automobile company. They were made by large and small manufacturers scattered all over the country, who shipped these parts to the auto factory where they were assembled into a car. Those same companies make the replacement parts sold by your dealer as well as by the independent parts stores. It is true that some of the parts are made by the auto company, but only the company knows which ones. Because prices of parts are often lower at the parts store than at the car dealer, I suggest you try the parts store first.

For some of you, neither alternative is useful. Perhaps you live 50 miles from the nearest dealer and parts store. Mail order may be your best option. There are thousands of companies who do business largely or totally by mail, supplying brand-name parts often at discount prices. Many specialty parts can only be obtained from them. A quick trip through any car or truck magazine will show you dozens of ads for repair and modification parts. Some of the companies deal only in suspension or engine parts. Some specialize in one or two makes of cars or trucks. Others are full-service companies, selling almost any part you might need.

There is a natural reluctance to send your money to a company hundreds of miles away. Admittedly, there may be a slight risk. However, if you deal with companies that continue to advertise in the same magazines over a period of several years, there is practically no risk. Mail fraud is a federal offense with severe penalties. Most magazines refuse to carry ads from companies with a high rate of reader complaint. If the part I needed was best available from a mail-order company in Turkey Crossing, New Mexico, and their ads had appeared in a reputable magazine over the past year, I would order without hesitation.

If you live near a city or metropolitan area, you will have a variety of discount stores nearby. Many of these carry at least some parts for the more popular models of cars and light trucks. Mufflers, exhaust pipes, shocks, wheels, tires, ignition parts, and various accessories can nearly always be found in discount stores. If the part has a brand-name you recognize, it is probably good quality. I would be reluctant to buy a brand I did not recognize.

There is another problem that has become widespread in the last few years. Counterfeit parts made in various Far-East countries have been found on the shelves of many parts stores. Even the experts have been fooled in some instances. These parts come in boxes that are near duplicates of those used by well-known companies. The only way you can protect yourself is to be as certain as possible that the part is what it claims to be. Look for quality of machining commensurate with what you expect from the brand-name.

The following is a discussion of some specific types of parts and where they can be located. The companies named are either ones I have successfully done business with or companies that I feel confident in recommending because of their reputations.

PARTS, HARDWARE, AND DISCOUNT STORES

Local hardware stores are good sources for tools and smaller parts such as hoses, wiring, light bulbs, fuses, and some exhaust system parts. Most hardware stores will carry at least two grades of quality in tools. They will have a line of top quality with recognizable brand names and another line of bargain tools. As mentioned earlier, bargain tools usually aren't.

Other items such as bulbs, hoses, clamps, and so forth can usually be bought without regard for brands. Hoses are hoses and clamps are clamps. I'm certain that some companies will not agree with that statement.

Discount stores such as K-Mart, Walmart, Shopco, and the other large regionals and nationals can be depended on for middle quality items in accessories. They also carry full lines of "mouse milk" and other fluids. With minor exceptions, I would not expect top quality in their wrenches and other hand tools. However, most of them carry Black and Decker power tools. If you need a sander or electric drill, these are good sources.

In many parts of the country, particularly in medium size cities in farming areas, there is a type of discount store catering to the small fleet and farming businesses. These stores are good sources for tools and some parts. Most of them have reasonable quality shocks and exhaust system parts as well as batteries and brand-name lubricants. Many of them carry tires with the brand-name Duralon. These tires are made by one of the major tire manufacturers and distributed to the discount chains. I have used Duralon tires for several years with only one instance of a problem. One new tire was out of round. They replaced it with no difficulty.

Auto parts stores come in two flavors, standard and discount. Both are likely to have top quality tools and brand-name filters, lubricants, and parts. Except for price, I have found little difference among them. Some of the discount parts stores also stock performance equipment. One in my area stocks Weiand intake manifolds and superchargers, Holley carburetors, and MSD ignition systems as well as other name-brands.

Parts stores tend to be regional chains. For the most part, they stock only top quality parts and tools. Many of their parts are made by the same companies that sell to the car companies. Often they will have catalogs for the more esoteric parts, such as computer ignitions and spark advance controls, that are not stocked. I've not found one that was not willing to special order for me. Because of the competition from the discount parts stores, many of these regionals discount heavily. That's especially true if you buy from them regularly and they get to recognize you. It's easy to convince them that you should get a professional discount.

The parts stores often either have or are associated with auto machine shops. These shops perform the kinds of work that require expensive equipment that you couldn't afford. Such jobs as facing valves and valve seats, turning brake drums and rotors, surfacing heads, grinding crankshafts, or boring cylinders are their specialties. Some also offer a balancing service to assure that your rebuilt engine runs free of vibration.

MAIL ORDER

For our purposes, mail-order stores fall into two groups: general and specialty. I'll discuss the general mail-order store first. Sears Roebuck is generally recognized as the epitome of mail-order or catalog stores. In addition to their general household and clothing merchandise, Sears sells a wide variety of items useful to the car buff. Their hand tools are as good as anyone's and carry a lifetime guarantee. Sears handles a full line of most repair parts from shocks and wheel bearings to complete engines and transmissions. They are also a good source for such customizing parts as seats, driving lights, wheels, and dress-up items. Sears carries some Edelbrock intake manifolds and camshafts as well as Rancho shocks and suspension parts.

Sears retail stores in many areas stock at least some of the parts listed in their catalogs. I have very little to complain about in their tires and batteries. The line of Sears tires is as broad as most regular tire stores. They carry their own brand, made by a major tire manufacturer, and some Michelin sizes.

Penney's catalog carries many of the same categories of items as Sears but in different brands. If you check their catalog you will recognize the names instantly. In the past, Penney's has operated retail auto stores in some locations. I'm not aware of any at the present time.

Nearly every magazine stand in the country has a J.C. Whitney catalog for sale in the car magazine area. Whitney, P.O. Box 8410, Chicago, IL 60680, has a variety of catalogs listing about everything you could want in tools, parts, and customizing items. Order from them once and you will continue to receive catalogs on a frequent basis for years. The quality of items I have received from Whitney has varied. Some items have been good, some not so good. To be honest, I would be reluctant to order engine parts or other items in which I wanted top quality. Where top precision is not required, I would have no reluctance.

SPECIALTY MAIL ORDER

There are some items that can only be obtained from mail-order stores specializing in those items. If you want suspension parts different from stock items, you will almost have to find a specialty shop. Some parts are only available from the manufacturer. Browse through any issue of *4 Wheel & Off-Road, Four Wheeler, Hot Rod*, or similar magazines, and you will find a fantastic wealth of companies advertising nearly anything you can imagine in car and light truck parts and accessories. Most of them will send you a catalog for the asking.

There are some companies that deserve special mention. If you're thinking about superchargers, the names Edelbrock, Weiand, B & M, and Latham are important. Weiand, Edelbrock, and B & M build a variety of superchargers for many popular engines. Their superchargers are all of the Roots type. This kind of supercharger has a long history. The Roots blower originally was designed as a water mill to replace conventional waterwheels. It didn't work very well, but was found to be useful for pumping large quantities of air at low pressure for blast furnaces. Much later the Roots blower became an integral part of two-cycle diesel engines built by General Motors. Hot rodders adapted it to supercharge gasoline engines, and the rest is history. Weiand, Edelbrock, B & M, and others sell rebuilt GM blowers and their own smaller designs. Each claims engineering advantages. All work well and do exactly what they claim to do.

The Latham supercharger is completely different from the Roots blower in design and operation. It uses an axial flow compressor similar to the compressor in an aircraft jet engine. Compared with a Roots blower, the output of a Latham supercharger is cooler and denser. Latham claims a significantly lower drive power requirement than a Roots blower. If you are thinking of adding a supercharger, the Latham is certainly worthy of consideration.

B & M Automotive Products
9152 Independence Ave.
Chatsworth, CA 91311

Edelbrock
2700 California St.
Torrance, CA 90509-2936

Latham Supercharger
31275 La Baya, Unit D
Westlake Village, CA 91362

Weiand Automotive Industries
P.O. Box 65977
Los Angeles, CA 90065

Turbochargers accomplish the same result as the superchargers mentioned above. They just do it differently. There are several names prominent in turbochargers. I especially like the engineering approach of Gale Banks Engineering, but others are worthy of consideration.

Gale Banks Engineering
546 Duggan Ave.
Azusa, CA 91702

BAE Division of Turdyne
3032 Kashiwa
Torrance, CA 90505

Crane Cams
P.O. Box 160
Hallandale, FL 33009

Rajay Industries
P.O. Box 207
Long Beach, CA 90801

Ak Miller Garage
9236 Bermudez St.
Pico Rivera, CA 90660

Spearco Performance Products
10936 S. La Cienega Blvd.
Inglewood, CA 90304

Turbo Systems
1817 N. Medina Line Rd.
Akron, OH 44313

This list is by no means exhaustive. Check any issue of *Hot Rod* or *Turbo* magazines for others.

Several companies manufacture some sort of advanced electronic ignition system ranging from special coils to computer ignition systems. Most of these can be purchased or ordered at your local parts store. I list the addresses of two companies whose literature you should consult when selecting the unit best suited to your use.

Jacobs Electronics
3327 Verdugo Rd.
Los Angeles, CA 90065

MSD Ignitions
Autotronic Controls Corporation
1490 Henry Brennan Dr.
El Paso, TX 79936

Companies manufacturing performance intake manifolds and related items abound. There are too many to list. I especially like these.

Crane Cams, Inc. (Also carry adjustable vacuum advance)
100 N.W. Ninth Terrace
Hallandale, FL 33009

Edelbrock
2700 California St.
Torrance, CA 90509-2936

Weiand Automotive Industries
P.O. Box 65977
Los Angeles, CA 90065

Suspension parts are also available from many sources. There are numerous companies making shock absorbers, but these are generally available from local parts stores. Custom items, such as antiroll bars, springs, urethane bushings for shocks and springs, steering stabilizers, and lift kits might have to be ordered through a catalog. Check the various enthusiast magazines for sources in addition to the two below.

Rancho Suspension
P.O. Box 5429
Long Beach, CA 90805

Suspension Techniques
1854 Belcroft Ave.
South El Monte, CA 91733

The following reference materials might be useful for additional reading. They are readily available from most book stores or can be ordered from the publishers.

Ganahl, Pat. *A Do-it-yourself Guide to Street Supercharging*. Brea, CA: S-A Design Publishing Co.

Jacobs, Christopher. *The Doctor's Guide to Automotive Ignition*. Los Angeles: Jacobs Technical Publications.

MacInnes, Hugh. *Turbochargers*. Tucson, AZ: H.P. Books, 1976.

Puhn, Fred. *How to Make Your Car Handle*. Tucson, AZ: H.P. Books.

Roe, Doug. *Rochester Carburetors*. Tucson, AZ: H.P. Books, 1986.

Index

Index

146

Other Bestsellers From TAB

□ **CAR DESIGN: STRUCTURE & ARCHITECTURE—Jan P. Norbye**

Here's an inside look at automotive design—from the drawing board to the showroom floor . . . from the horseless carriage to the compact cars of the '80s! This book examines the reasons behind the positioning of the seats, engines, and other necessary elements, and how these choices affect the body styling freedom of the body designer. 384 pp., 315 illus.

Paper $15.95   **Hard $20.50**
Book No. 2104

□ **UNDERSTANDING AUTOMOTIVE SPECIFICATIONS AND DATA—James Flammang**

Do you feel like you have to be a mathematician to figure out all the numbers involved in automotive repair? Then you need this invaluable guide that explains all the numerical concepts you need to do tune-ups, overhauls, or adjustments, plus details on engine size, power, and economy. Amateur mechanics, and automobile enthusiasts will find this guide indispensable. 208 pp.m 123 illus.

Paper $10.95   **Hard $12.95**
Book No. 2116

□ **BEST OF BAX: Collected Columns from Car & Driver—Gordon Baxter**

This book is packed with delightful tales based upon one of the author's many loves—cars. In his funny, down-to-earth style, Baxter describes automobiles he has had experience with during his long career as a self-proclaimed "automobilic," from the days of his wild youth to present day. Into these stories Baxter introduces humorous accounts of other drivers, car dealers, and his native state of Texas and its drivers and personalities. 240 pp., Illustrated

Paper $11.95   **Hard $13.95**
Book No. 2119

□ **FORD ESCORT/MERCURY LYNX CARS (1981-1984): DO-IT-YOURSELF CAR CARE—Larry W. Carley**

This guide covers all bases on maintenance and repair within the realm of the automobile owner . . . shows you how you can do it all yourself without the use of expensive or specialized tools and equipment. Reviewed in detail are engine, transmission, electrical and ignition systems, brakes, chassis, suspension, tires, air-conditioning systems, exhaust systems, winterizing, and more! 240 pp., 223 illus.

Paper $11.95   **Hard $13.95**
Book No. 2133

□ **CONSUMER'S GUIDE TO SUCCESSFUL CAR SHOPPING: How To Drive Away Your Best Deal—Peter Sessler**

Expert advice that will save you hundreds of dollars and hours of wasted time when buying a car—new, used, classic, foreign, or domestic! Sessler gives you facts on new car mileage, options, and performance, a used car guide and data on your legal rights, warranties, service contracts, leasing, insurance, lemon laws, how to buy an import, and more! 128 pp., 67 illus.

Paper $10.95   **Hard $15.95**
Book No. 2117

□ **LIVING ON WHEELS: The Complete Guide to Motorhomes—John Boardman**

Covers buying, renting, operating, servicing, and maintaining motorhomes and their installed equipment. Here's a wealth of expert tips and guidance on how to make a wise and informed choice when selecting your motorhome. With the help of this guide you can determine and decide for yourself which motorhome designs provide the safety, dependability, durability, reliability, and economy that you require and demand. In addition, if you already own a motorhome, you'll find all the information you need here to keep yours looking and running like new! 304 pp., 164 illus.

Paper $9.95   **Hard $19.95**
Book No. 2118

□ **CADILLAC—AMERICA'S LUXURY CAR—Robert C. Ackerson**

Cadillac popularity continues to grow. Now, carefully and vividly documented in this new book for its thousands of owners and admirers worldwide, is the Cadillac's post-World War II history. *Cadillac— America's Luxury Car* examines virtually every Cadillac manufactured from 1945 through 1987 and includes photographs of all models made through 1989. This lavishly illustrated volume represents a complete look at this remarkable luxury car. 368 pp., Over 275 illustrations.

Paper $29.95   **Hard $39.95**
Book No. 2120

□ **THE ELECTROPLATER'S HANDBOOK—C.W. Ammen**

If you want to plate any kind of object for any purpose, this is the guide to have! It's an invaluable guide whether you're a model railroad builder, auto or antique restorer, amateur jeweler, coin collector, science buff, radio and electronics builder, silversmith, metal caster, artist, sculptor, potter, small manufacturer, stained glass worker, inventor, or even a parent who wants to bronze baby shoes! 272 pp., 121 illus.

Paper $14.95   **Hard $18.95**
Book No. 2610

Other Bestsellers From TAB

☐ **THE FIBERGLASS REPAIR AND CONSTRUCTION HANDBOOK—2nd Edition—Jack Wiley**

Jack Wiley adds to an already exceptional manual in this second edition. Easy to follow, this guide takes you from choosing your tools through the final touches on simple and complex projects. Absolutely no prior experience is required. Step-by-step instructions cover everything from materials selection to the final lamination process and safety precautions,. The author includes practice exercises on how to work with glass cloth, mat, core materials, and resins before starting you on repairs or the customizing of a boat or car. 288 pp., 303 illus.

Paper $17.95   **Hard $21.95**
Book No. 2779

☐ **DIESEL ENGINE MECHANICS—Wayne A. Kelm**

Packed with line drawings and illustrated diagrams, *Diesel Engine Mechanics* covers the construction, operation, and service of diesel engines commonly found in today's automotive, light construction, agricultural, industrial and marine type vehicles and equipment up to 100 hp. This guide can save hundreds of dollars by showing how you can maintain, troubleshoot, and repair these engines yourself. It also provides the sound, general foundation that is needed to begin a career in diesel mechanics. 288 pp., 265 illus.

Paper $16.95   **Hard $21.95**
Book No. 2780

Send $1 for the new TAB Catalog describing over 1300 titles currently in print and receive a coupon worth $1 off on your next purchase from TAB.

(In PA, NY, and ME add applicable sales tax. Orders subject to credit approval. Orders outside U.S. must be prepaid with international money orders in U.S. dollars.)

*Prices subject to change without notice.

▬▬▬▬▬▬▬▬▬▬▬▬▬▬▬▬▬▬▬▬▬▬▬▬▬▬▬▬▬▬▬▬▬▬▬▬▬▬

To purchase these or any other books from TAB, visit your local bookstore, return this coupon, or call toll-free 1-800-822-8158 (In PA and AK call 1-717-794-2191).

Product No.	Hard or Paper	Title	Quantity	Price

☐ Check or money order enclosed made payable to TAB BOOKS Inc.

Charge my   ☐ VISA   ☐ MasterCard   ☐ American Express

Acct. No. _____ Exp. _____

Signature _____

Please Print
Name _____

Company _____

Address _____

City _____

State _____ Zip _____

Subtotal	
Postage/Handling ($5.00 outside U.S.A. and Canada)	$2.50
In PA, NY, and ME add applicable sales tax	
TOTAL	

Mail coupon to:

TAB BOOKS Inc.
Blue Ridge Summit
PA 17294-0840

BC